REFLECTIONS
ON A LIFE IN SPORT

With best wishes to
Mike McNamee.

Sam Ramsamy

Olympia - 21 September 2016

Published by Greenhouse

First published in 2004

ISBN 0 620 32251 9

Produced for Greenhouse by The Publishing Partnership, 30 Keerom Street, Cape Town, 8001

Cover photograph by Nardus Nel
Cover design by The Publishing Partnership
Reproduction by Hirt & Carter, Cape Town
Printed and bound by ABC Press, Epping

REFLECTIONS
ON A LIFE IN SPORT

Sam Ramsamy

with Edward Griffiths

GREENHOVSE

This book is dedicated to Helga, my wife,
and all the activists, recognised
and unrecognised, who contributed
to the destruction of apartheid in sport.

CONTENTS

FOREWORD

by
Thabo Mbeki
President, Republic of South Africa

In his book *The Murdoch Archipelago*, Bruce Page reports that the English novelist Anthony Trollope visited Australia in 1871. He writes: "Trollope may be thought a reliable witness, for he noticed, in addition to the urge to publish, other durable national attributes, such as an addiction to competitive sport and a collective, hair-trigger resentment of alien criticism, however modestly offered."

Had Trollope come to South Africa a hundred years after he had visited Australia, he would have said the same thing about white South Africa, that among other things, its durable national attributes were "addiction to competitive sport and a collective, hair-trigger resentment of alien criticism, however modestly offered."

That shared addiction to competitive sport, which still seems to characterise both Australia and South Africa, was to turn into an intense area of international conflict, as the subject of this autobiography, Sam Ramsamy, and others, led a global struggle against apartheid sport.

It is certainly true that before this particular struggle assumed the intensity and international prominence it did, as the world escalated its campaign against apartheid South Africa, many among us did not fully appreciate the role and place of sport in human society.

The struggle that Sam Ramsamy and others led to deracialise sport in South Africa and more generally to defeat the apartheid system, ended our age of ignorance about what is clearly an important area of human activity, sport. The knowledge he helped us to acquire has stood us in good stead as we work to build the new South Africa towards whose birth Sam Ramsamy contributed so much.

In 1999, the outstanding New Zealand leader and activist against apartheid, Trevor Richards, published the fascinating book *Dancing on our Bones: New Zealand, South Africa, Rugby and Racism*. The title of the book is based on what Henderson Tapela said in New Zealand in 1970, where he was a student and President of the African Students' Association. Reflecting the intensity of feeling against playing sport with racist South Africa, he advised New Zealanders, "Don't go to South Africa to play the white teams, for if you do, you will be dancing on our bones."

The same Anthony Trollope who called on Australia in 1871, also visited one of the oldest Mission Schools in our country, Lovedale Institution. To celebrate its centenary in 1941, one of its distinguished Principals, the Reverend RHW Shepherd, published a history of the institution entitled *Lovedale, South Africa: The Story of a Century, 1841 – 1941*.

Shepherd did not disclose what Trollope said during his visit to Lovedale with regard to addiction to competitive sport, or any other subject for that matter. However, Shepherd discussed the role of sport in the "civilising" mission that the Scottish Presbyterians had set themselves when they established Lovedale Missionary Institution. He wrote: "Lovedale is concerned with the whole man, body, mind and spirit. With some 700 young people as boarders constantly within the Institution, special steps must be taken for the safeguarding of health through games and other recreation. To look over Lovedale's Annual Report in any year is to see a network of activities centring on the sports' field: athletics, rugby, soccer, cricket, netball, and tennis…

"Recreation is a matter of supreme importance in the eyes of those responsible for Lovedale. Many of the amusements of the unconverted Bantu are incompatible with Christian purity of life, and so have to be abandoned by those embracing Christianity. But youth is youth the world over, and therefore among the Bantu, as among all other races, provision must be made for social activities, healthy exercise and the profitable employment of leisure. What is and what is not Christian in this connection is a burning question in rural areas and urban centres.

"A missionary of long experience recently declared… 'We look to Lovedale to send out students who will do much to create and encourage healthier and better forms of social fellowship, including games.' Such considerations emphasise the importance of sport in Lovedale…"

To understand this matter properly, we should refer to an 1841 "Report of the Glasgow Missionary Society", the organisation responsible for the establishment of Lovedale. Looking forward to a century later, the Society said: "Our brethren of the Mission shall then have also ceased from their toil, and they and we shall, we trust, be permitted to rejoice together (in

Heaven). And may we not add, that there will be in the same company some of the first fruits of Kaffreland, as earnests of that greater multitude who shall yet be gathered to Christ out of that dark and degraded land? It is at least probable that a hundred years hence Kaffreland will be a Christian country, and that the Lovedale Institution, or some other to which it may give rise, will be sending forth its hundreds of sons and daughters of Ethiopia as messengers of the Cross, eastwards and northwards, into countries of which we know not as yet even the name."

The then Minister of Education and of Finance, the well-known "liberal" Jan H Hofmeyr, wrote the Introduction to Shepherd's history of Lovedale. He said: "When sometimes, in none too happy phrase, it is urged, in support of a policy of keeping the Natives down, that we must make South Africa safe for European civilisation, it is well that it should be pointed out that it is the missionaries who above all others have made South Africa safe for European civilisation. It is not only the Black man, it is also the White man, who should thank God for the missionaries."

The missionaries of the Glasgow Missionary Society saw it as their duty to civilise Kaffirland, "that dark and degraded land". They looked forward to Lovedale producing black Christian missionaries who would spread "civilisation" and the Gospel to other African countries "of which we know not as yet even the name."

Lovedale itself thought it must produce these "Bantu" missionaries in part by training its students in the European sports codes, so that they abandon "amusements of the unconverted Bantu (that) are incompatible with Christian purity of life." Jan Hofmeyr advised "the White man" to thank God for the missionaries, and assured white South Africa that all missionary activity in Lovedale and elsewhere "made South Africa safe for European civilisation".

All this communicates the message that sport in our country amounted to much more than playing games! Seemingly, the very success of the "civilising mission" of imperial Europe depended on the "addiction to competitive sport" noted by Anthony Trollope when he visited Australia in 1871, 30 years after the establishment of the Lovedale Missionary Institution.

If RHW Shepherd is to be believed, presumably the British, Irish, Dutch, French and Germans who emigrated from Europe to Australia and

South Africa under varying circumstances, were already civilised by the time they set foot in their new homelands, already inducted into European sport. Because thousands of kilometres separated them from their ancestral homes, perhaps their addiction to competitive sport constituted a deeply felt and needed affirmation that they were European and civilised, despite the distance of their new habitats from civilised Europe!

As reported by Trevor Richards, when the long-time leader of white South African Rugby, Danie Craven, was told of the extent of opposition in New Zealand to the then forthcoming 1981 tour of the Springboks, he said: "I can hardly believe it of New Zealand. To me it is incredible that the nation I know so well has succumbed to that... You know, in 1937 and again in 1956, I preached from the pulpits in New Zealand, not once but dozens of times...I believe – I really in my soul believe – that their love of rugby will triumph over their love of demonstrating. There may be demonstrations at the start, but they will soon peter out."

But of course Danie Craven was wrong. The demonstrations did not peter out. Even the love of rugby could not stop thousands of New Zealanders from demonstrating in favour of nonracial sport in our country and freedom for the oppressed black millions. The reason Danie Craven could not understand or predict the intense opposition to the 1981 New Zealand Springbok Tour was that he proceeded from the firm knowledge of the bonds that existed among the white Dominions of the British Empire – Australia, New Zealand and South Africa.

Together they represented European outposts in the "dark and degraded lands" of which the Glasgow Missionary Society wrote. Together, they felt an instinctive sense of solidarity. Together, they loved rugby and revelled in competing and winning and losing against one another, precisely as a way of strengthening their bonds.

As the campaign for the isolation of apartheid South Africa gathered pace in Australia and the world, a future Australian Federal Member of Parliament, Robert Fenton, formed an organisation called WARD, War Against Recreational Disruption. He angrily proclaimed: "In the abuse and debasement of sport and culture by disruption, encouragement is given to subversive elements working for the overthrow of democratic government. The danger is accelerated by the inroads of a spurious morality designed to appeal to the disenchanted members of Western Society... A doomsday faces our culture if apathy is not overcome. The unremitting propaganda campaign against European Africa is harnessing innocent people to agitate for the very situation that offers them no opportunity to endure as free men. Manipulative forces are persuading the Free World to betray principle, abandon Law and make concessions in the face of coercion..."

This is how Danie Craven also saw the world. And this is what he knew of the other White Dominions – that together they represented "western society", which, among other things, was determined to protect "European Africa" from "subversive elements" that threatened the "culture" of the "Free World".

But what was to come, despite the Fentons and the Cravens, was reflected in the comments of Morné du Plessis, an outstanding Springbok rugby player and captain. He has said: "Going to New Zealand and Australia in 1971 as a 21-year-old and seeing the demonstrations against us and wondering quietly – but not seriously because life is fantastic and you're on tour and you're being fêted and dined and you're a Springbok and you're playing rugby and that's all you want to do. But you're thinking, can so many people so far away from us be so angry with us? Can it be that they're all wrong? Because we were told that they were all wrong."

A leading activist against the 1971 Springbok tour of Australia that Morné du Plessis spoke about, Meredith Burgman, said: "(The campaign against the tour) certainly changed Australians' attitude towards South Africa and apartheid, and we stopped being seen as South Africa's white brother across the sea, which really was how we were looked on by the world, and how we really looked at ourselves. So it changed that attitude."

What troubled Morné du Plessis was the dawning realisation that "South Africa's brother across the sea" was turning his back on "European Africa". On the contrary, Danie Craven continued to entertain the illusion that this could never happen, given that white South Africa, white Australia and white New Zealand saw one another as "brothers across the sea". Because of this, he was convinced that the demonstrations that worried Morné du Plessis reflected nothing more than a peculiar "love of demonstrating".

In his autobiography, *The Last Trek – A New Beginning*, former President FW de Klerk wrote about "how deeply white South Africans loved international sport". He said, "As the sporting net closed more tightly around us, all we could do was to provide financial aid to help sport organisations to continue their struggle and, sometimes, even to arrange rebel tours."

Some of the New Zealand All Blacks team undertook one of these rebel tours of South Africa in 1986. A reporter wrote, "A rebel rugby team of All Blacks, calling themselves the Cavaliers, after lies and deceit, sneak out of New Zealand and are defeated 3-1 in a series against the Springboks during a tour of South Africa."

Sam Ramsamy and his colleagues involved in nonracial sport understood how deeply white South Africa loved to participate in international sports, even to the point of relying on lies and deceit to achieve their goals. They understood that if they cut off white South Africans from international sport, the message would get through to the whites who "loved international sport", that the apartheid sport and the apartheid system they saw as their guarantee for the defence and perpetuation of "European Africa", were precisely the things that threatened their survival.

To isolate apartheid sport was to cut off the South African European outpost from the Europe of which it saw itself as an extension. It was to deny it the comfort of communion with the White Dominions, and the strength it drew from this association with its "brothers across the sea".

It was to plant the seed in the minds of young Afrikaners such as Morné du Plessis, even at the height of the arrogant confidence of white power, that, perhaps, not all was well with the South Africa that prided itself on the prowess of the Springboks.

But beyond this, the international campaign that Sam Ramsamy led shook up especially the countries and the sports communities with which "European Africa" felt a close affinity. It deeply affected those who had been accustomed and pleased to welcome on tour, fête, dine and commune with white South African rugby players and cricketers as friends and members of one family.

As these sought to protect a comfortable relationship informed by notions of kith and kin, and a shared obligation to defend themselves against the "dark and degraded lands", they did things that were out of the ordinary. Commenting on what happened as she and other Australians demonstrated in 1971 against the touring Springbok team, Verity Burgman, sister to

Meredith, said: "(The police) dragged us off the ground. The crowd (of spectators) shouted, yelled, screamed abuse at us. I was very nervous. The police were frightening, but perhaps not as frightening as the rugby supporters. This was an intensely polarised time in Australian history, when the old-fashioned forces of the world as it used to be were ranged behind their love of rugby, against the new forces of anti-apartheid, anti-racism, what you could generally term the new social movements that were developing then. Although we appeared to be a beleaguered minority, we were the ones that won out."

The Premier of Queensland, Bjelke-Petersen, even declared a state of emergency to protect the touring Springboks. The trade unions immediately organised a 24-hour strike. With extended emergency powers, the police dealt harshly with anti-apartheid activists described as "long-haired protesters."

Trevor Richards wrote that commentators said that because of the Springbok tour, Australia had become a country "pitted against itself".

The same thing happened when the people of New Zealand stood up to oppose the 1981 Springbok tour. The government deployed the army and the air force to confront the anti-apartheid demonstrators. The police were issued with long batons, which they used to assault the demonstrators after one match had had to be abandoned. New Zealand had never experienced such overwhelming use of force against peaceful protests. A Presbyterian Church leader, John Murray, said: "This is not New Zealand – this is a nightmare!"

But so stubborn was the New Zealand Rugby Football Union about the need to support "the brothers across the sea", that despite the fact that the 1981 Springbok tour had plunged New Zealand into a crisis, it nevertheless decided that the All Blacks should tour South Africa in 1985. In the end, this tour was prohibited by the New Zealand courts, which responded to an injunction that was sought by two New Zealand lawyers.

In his judgement, Justice Casey said: "Those opposed (to the tour) cannot be brushed aside as irresponsible trouble-makers or publicity seekers, as some of the evidence and opinions from the (Rugby) Union suggests… Most of the reasons (for opposing the tour) may have no direct connection with benefiting local rugby. But taken together, they must result in a groundswell of public opinion exasperated or angry with the Union's stance, and very concerned about re-opening the scars of 1981… The interest of the public and of the nation in not having the tour go ahead is a most potent factor…There is also the risk of violence and bloodshed – even loss of life – to black Africans."

Together with Henderson Tapela, Justice Casey said, "Don't go to South Africa to play the white teams, for if you do, you will be dancing on (the) bones (of black Africans)." Trevor Richards reports that even in 1996, 15 years after the events of 1981, which had proved to be deeply traumatic for New Zealand society, "the ghost of 1981 had (not) been laid to rest", and observed that it was perhaps "too soon for a spectre of such significance to twentieth-century New Zealand to find its peace".

To contribute to the effort to lay the ghost of 1981 to rest, to heal "the scars of 1981", the future Prime Minister of New Zealand, Helen Clark, herself an anti-apartheid activist, moved a resolution in the New Zealand parliament, which, fortunately, was approved unanimously. In part the reso-lution said: "The House acknowledges the importance of the contribution made by New Zealand citizens and organisations over the period 1948-1990 to national and internal campaigns against apartheid; recognises that their contribution not only gave great encouragement and support to those in South Africa campaigning against apartheid, but was also responsible for earning New Zealand enduring international respect; resolves to close this chapter of our history relating to the old South Africa and to move forward together to a new, positive, practical and compassionate relationship with the new South Africa."

The global campaign to isolate apartheid sport, ably led by Sam Ramsamy and his colleagues, won many victories. South Africa was sus-pended from the 1964 Olympics and expelled from the Olympic movement in 1970. FIFA expelled South Africa from world soccer in 1976. The 1978 Springbok tour of the UK and the 1979 Wallabies tour of South Africa were both cancelled.

In 1975 the UN General Assembly adopted a resolution on apartheid in sport, calling on all sports organisations to uphold the Olympic principle of non-discrimination. In 1977 the Commonwealth Heads of Government Meeting (CHOGM) adopted the "Gleneagles Agreement", which resolved that all member states should take "every practical step to discourage contact or competition by their nationals with sporting organisations, teams or sportsmen from South Africa".

This highly informative autobiography of Sam Ramsamy reflects on these and many other victories in the struggle against apartheid sport and the apartheid regime. But the importance of this life history lies in more than the mere account of the events that occurred, in which Sam Ramsamy was a central player.

Interviewed about sports contacts between Australia and apartheid South Africa, Lloyd McDermott said, "One of the white players who was picked to play for Australia and refused to play against the all-white South African team…was counselled by one of the Australian selectors that he'd been the victim of a communist conspiracy."

The Australian, Meredith Burgman, said, "One of the arguments that kept being raised by the apologists for the South Africans was 'Well why don't you clean up your own backyard? You know, look what's happening to Aborigines'. And in a funny way that was very healthy for the way in which the media had been treating Aboriginal issues. Of course the media started then to look at Aboriginal issues, and young Aboriginal activists of the time were very prominent in the demonstrations against the Springboks… and so I think it did start raising the whole issue of white Australia's relationship with Aboriginal Australia."

Responding to pressures to support the Gleneagles Agreement, the New Zealand Prime Minister, Robert Muldoon, said, "I certainly am not going to compromise the Government's standards on the freedom of the individual in order to get a black athlete to (the 1978) Edmonton (Commonwealth Games)." Muldoon sought to hide his racist positions behind liberal rhetoric about individual freedom, as had done the Australian rugby selector, when he tried to exploit the prevalent anti-communism of the day, and as had done Fenton, when he referred to the "culture" of the "Free World."

But Sam Ramsamy and others relentlessly stripped away what, in other circumstances, Winston Churchill had described as "a bodyguard of lies". Once this was done, what emerged was the ugly face of racism in South Africa and everywhere else in the world.

The removal of the bodyguard of lies, built to protect apartheid racism in South Africa, educated the millions across the world who love sport, about the way in which lies were used in their countries everyday, to hide from the people the truth about many things, well beyond apartheid racism in South Africa.

By empowering millions across the globe to see beyond the public lies and deceit that were part of their daily lives, such as those used to prepare for the Cavaliers rebel tour, Sam Ramsamy's campaign against apartheid sport opened the door to these millions to discover the truth for themselves, and reclaim the responsibility to build a better world for themselves and all humanity.

Tony Abrahams, a member of the Wallabies team that toured South Africa in 1969 said: "From the moment you got off the plane (in South Africa), you were conscious of this grotesque compromise in being there…" No human being with any conscience could fail to ask themselves the question whether they were willing to enter into this grotesque compromise, and what benefit there would be in playing sport over the bones of those killed by apartheid, despite the grave warnings given by Henderson Tapela and Justice Casey.

Verity Burgman said: "The old fashioned forces of the world as it used to be were ranged behind their love of rugby, against the new forces of… anti-racism, what you could generally term the new social movements that were developing then."

The reason it took a long time to "lay the ghost of 1981" in New Zealand was because the old fashioned forces of the world, the screaming rugby supporters who had frightened Verity Burgman more than the frightening police, sustained the conviction that they had lost a battle to the new forces represented by the new social movements, but not the war. This was a war not just about apartheid racism, but also about the survival of a particular world-view and vision of the future of humanity.

It has been a privilege to know and work with Sam Ramsamy for many years now. It says much about him and about the nobility of the human soul that one such as he, a humble South African, born into an oppressive society and into humble surroundings, could walk the globe and make the impact he did, as one of the midwives of democratic South Africa and a catalyst of new thinking in the world.

Quite naturally, in the years since the international sports boycott was lifted, Sam Ramsamy has had the duty to lead the challenging process of building non-racial sport in our country, ensuring that the addiction to competitive sport serves to unite our people in a spirit of national reconciliation, rather than racial division and conflict.

As President of the National Olympic Committee of South Africa and member of the International Olympic Committee, he has had the responsibility to oversee the process of building and sending out to all countries new 'sons and daughters of Ethiopia', as messengers of our people's hopes for peace, friendship and solidarity among the youth and peoples of the world. Nelson Mandela visited New Zealand in 1995. Commenting on the cancellation of one of the All Blacks-Springbok matches during the 1981 tour, because of the struggle waged by the New Zealand anti-apartheid movement while he and others were still on Robben Island, he said, "It felt like the sun coming out."

As South Africans privileged to have in our midst a patriot and humanist as distinguished as Sam Ramsamy is, we will continue to count on him to help our people to achieve new victories as they engage the struggle for a better life for all. The new successes he will surely help our people to achieve will, once more, make the millions of our people proclaim that they too feel like the sun is coming out!

FOREWORD

by
Jacques Rogge
President, International Olympic Committee

The Olympic Movement would not be in the position it enjoys today in our society without men like Sam Ramsamy.

Throughout his life, Sam Ramsamy has made his own the fundamental values of sport in general and Olympism in particular, which are mutual understanding, tolerance and solidarity between peoples. His autobiography recounts the story of a man who has never stopped fighting for human dignity and human rights in order to build sport without barriers in South Africa.

He has used his firm convictions to serve his country and the Olympic Movement. He played a key role in the readmission of the South African NOC to the Olympic fold after a 28-year absence.

After serving as Chairman of the South African Non-Racial Olympic Committee (SANROC) from 1976 to 1990, the following year he became the first President of an all-race NOC, which made its return to the Olympic stage at the Games of the XXV Olympiad in Barcelona, in 1992. He was also a member of the IOC 'Apartheid and Olympism' Commission from 1989 to 1991.

Since becoming an IOC member in 1995, he has brought all his know-how and sports leadership experience to bear within several commissions (Sport and Environment, IOC 2000, Culture and Olympic Education, Press and Olympic Programme).

The IOC is proud to have Sam Ramsamy, a defender of the Olympic ideal, as one of its members.

To my colleague and friend Sam Ramsamy, I express the Olympic family's affection and recognition of the lessons in courage and determination recounted here in his book, *Reflections on a Life in Sport*.

FOREWORD

by
Alan Knott-Craig
Group CEO, Vodacom

Vodacom is a company in pursuit of excellence – and to perhaps extend the Olympic motto, we have attempted to be faster, higher, stronger – and smarter! So, it is no coincidence that as a company born to the new South Africa, we immediately engaged with the National Olympic Committee of South Africa in 1994, to bolster the national effort in preparing our athletes for the acme in human sporting achievement – the Olympic Games.

And so our association with a stalwart of South African sport, Sam Ramsamy, began. Our first meeting at the rather spartan surrounds of the old Olympic House in Melrose was decisive. This was a man with whom we wanted to work – direct, honest and passionate about sport and the Olympic movement. We pledged our support with a handshake, and ten years on, we still cherish the association with NOCSA and our friendship with Sam Ramsamy.

And so it is a singular honour for Vodacom to support the publishing of Sam's biography. Sam has been a great servant of South Africa. Through his years in exile, he was a constant thorn in the side of the apartheid government, and was sometimes vilified in the local media.

He understood the primacy and potency of sport, and through the South African Non-Racial Olympic Committee he was able to play a lead role in the sports boycott. His view was that he did not want the government of the day to simulate a normal society through the hosting of rebel tours in South Africa. And so he was able to leverage off his skills and competencies in contributing to a democratic South Africa.

Now, we can add Sam's story to the history of sport in South Africa, particularly the re-unification effort in the late 1980s.

It simply would not be complete without it.

JUST CAUSE

It has been a just cause. Without seeming self-satisfied or smug, my conviction remains as strong today as it was 50 years ago. I honestly believed it then, and I honestly believe it now. Equal opportunity in South African sport: that has been the cause, the right of every South African to play sport and be eligible to represent their country, regardless of colour, race, religion, gender or wealth.

This is the goal I have pursued for most of my life, in fact almost all of it. For 35 years, this objective led me to campaign for the isolation of 'white' South African sport from international competition. For the past 15 years, I have worked within unified structures to make equal opportunity a reality.

As in any life, there have been successes and disappointments, good decisions and poor decisions, but it is with genuine sincerity that I am now able to reflect and conclude that, yes, it was a just cause.

There comes a time, when you have long passed 60 and the years seem to be fast accelerating towards your 70th birthday and hopefully beyond, when you feel the need to sit down and reflect on what you have done, to take stock. This book stems from a sense that I have reached this stage.

It is not a vehicle to settle old scores. In fact, perhaps surprisingly after a life where conflict and controversy seem to have hung around me, I don't particularly feel as though I have any scores to settle. There are no thorns in my side.

Jean-Claude Ganga, a close friend and a former International Olympic Committee (IOC) member from the Congo, always liked to tell a story from West Africa about a poor man who went to bathe in a village pond. Not long afterwards, a wealthy chap arrived at the same pond because he also wanted to bathe. The rich man undressed, laid down his fine clothes, and stepped into the water. Now, the poor man had watched all of this intently; and, in an instant, he rushed out of the pond, grabbed the rich man's clothes and ran away down the main street of the village.

"Be quick, sir," shouted a bystander at the pond. "If you chase him, you will surely catch him."

"No," the rich man replied. "I won't do that. Everyone in the village would see us, think one naked man is chasing another naked man, and say we are both fools. I will let him go."

I have tended to follow the same principle, preferring to let people say what they want about me, and just to leave them alone. Nobody ever comes clean out of a slanging match.

This book is also not an attempt to rewrite recent history. Of course, different people have different recollections of the same events, but all I can do is what I have done in these pages: to be rigorously honest and accurate in my memories, and faithfully set down what I saw, heard, felt, and thought.

If these are not the reasons for writing this book, you may well wonder what is the motivation?

First, I want people to know and understand what happened in the past, not simply in South African sport, but also in high-profile sporting bodies like the IOC and the Fédération International de Football Association (FIFA), and other major international federations.

I am keen for South Africans to know what sacrifices were made on their behalf, to know what was done to secure something which, happily, they seem to take for granted: their right to equal opportunities in sport.

"But, sir, history is boring," I hear the cry.

It's not the first time I have heard these words. During 12 years of working as a schoolteacher, first in South Africa and then in England, this view was expressed more than once. However, as I told the students back in the 1960s and 1970s, history is all we have to guide us in the future. Through the years, only fools have set it aside and ignored its lessons.

Second, I believe the wonderful wave of joy and enthusiasm, which has greeted South Africa's liberation and her progress as a democracy, has left certain individuals behind. To a greater or lesser extent, these people have remained unrecognised and unappreciated for their contribution.

Such oversights may have been unavoidable, and they have been made throughout the anti-apartheid struggle, but I am determined to honour the people who were prominent in the campaign to isolate apartheid sport.

These men and women helped South Africa during a difficult time, often at substantial cost to their own ambitions, and yet many have hardly been recognised and thanked in return.

Third, and lastly, it seems worthwhile to draw on 50 years of sporting experience and simply set down my thoughts, first on the major issues facing South African sport, and also on the challenges confronting the Olympic movement.

So, in the year when I plan to step down as President of the National Olympic Committee of South Africa (NOCSA), I have decided to put pen to paper; and I trust it will prove worthwhile.

My first reflection is that I know I could have chosen a much easier, less stressful – and less useful – life.

Devi, my late sister, is certainly one person who would have preferred me to choose a quieter existence. Our mother died when we were very young and we were extremely close. She supported me in everything I did, but I always sensed she would have liked me to be satisfied with living the best life possible under apartheid, keeping out of trouble, staying at home in Durban.

Many South Africans of Indian origin did exactly that, staying at home to look after their families and businesses.

Many didn't.

I trained as a teacher after school, and soon became heavily involved in sport, coaching swimming and soccer. However, it was impossible for me to ignore the effects of apartheid on sport and I was prompted to campaign for equal opportunities.

This was not a conscious career choice – nobody dreams of organising demonstrations and campaigning for change; for me, it was an instinctive reaction to naked injustice.

So, I started to attend meetings, and met people and slowly became involved in the struggle against apartheid sport.

In 1971, after helping to organise a student boycott of the so-called Republic Celebration Games, I was called aside by my head of department and told that I was under scrutiny and that, for my own safety, I should leave the country. I boarded a plane to England, and began two decades in exile.

Life was never easy during these years, and I missed family and friends, but, in many ways, I was fortunate.

The fact is I did not suffer as others suffered because I was neither imprisoned nor tortured; and, because I was always able to work, I never experienced extreme poverty.

There were severe sacrifices to be made, and tough times to withstand, and the odd bullet through the bedroom window, but, in general, my wife and I have been luckier than many.

And there have also been rewards… the sense of achievement in defeating apartheid sport and uniting five bodies to form NOCSA, the sense of pride in marching at the head of the readmitted South African team at the opening ceremony of the 1992 Summer Olympic Games in Barcelona. Such privilege is rare.

The experience of helping NOCSA grow into a stable, effective organisation, living up to its declared aim of 'Making Greater South Africans', has been tremendously gratifying.

Some people will like me, others will loathe me. Ever since my high-profile role in the anti-apartheid sports movement installed me as Public Enemy No 1 for many white South Africans, I have learned to accept a degree of notoriety as a fact of my life.

Conversely, most black South Africans appreciate my contribution to securing equal opportunities in sport.

Most important of all, I have tried to remain firm and constant in my opinions, and, humbly, I sleep well at night.

All in all, I am able to sit here at my desk, in the flat where my wife, Helga, and I live in Rosebank, Johannesburg, and reflect at ease upon an eventful life dedicated to a just cause.

BARRACKS

Our family's history in Africa, like that of many families who came from India, began on a false promise. My grandfather, Rungan, was living in the Madras Presidency, in the south of a country under British colonial rule, when he and his friends were approached by trading entrepreneurs. "Travel to Africa," they were told. "You will work in the Transvaal goldfields and make your fortune."

The prospect was tempting. Viewed from the dusty adversity of the subcontinent, everything that glittered did indeed look like gold, and my grandfather seized the opportunity. He agreed to lead his wife and three children across the Indian Ocean in search of a better life and perhaps previously unimagined riches. His dreams were soon shattered.

No sooner had the SS Umzinto docked in Durban, Rungan and his friends were informed that, in fact, there were no jobs for them in the Transvaal goldfields. Their only option, they were told, was to accept work in the sugar cane plantations near Tongaat. There was no other choice.

For some reason, at the start of the 20th century, Indians seemed to have earned a reputation for tending the fields. Ships packed with Indian labourers were dispatched to sugar plantations in Guyana, Mauritius, Reunion, Fiji, and Natal in South Africa.

So, stranded and bewildered far from home, my grandparents accepted their fate and calmly headed for the sugar plantation. In fact, they eventually settled so well in the Tongaat area that they had six more children. Two of these were boys who died young, which left one son to grow up alongside no fewer than six sisters. That solitary boy was my father.

He worked hard at school, learned to read and write and was rewarded with a job as a messenger boy at the Durban Municipality. His unusually high level of literacy swiftly earned him promotion to the position of clerk. At that time, my grandparents were living in a settlement specifically designated for Indian employees of the municipality and officially named Magazine Barracks.

This son of an immigrant labourer was making genuine progress. He decided to adopt 'Ramsamy' as a surname – at that time, people from the south of India tended to have only one name – and he married a gentle, intelligent woman named Rungama. On January 27th, 1938, there in the Barracks, they celebrated the birth of their first child, a son named Sambasivan… me.

A daughter, Devi, followed and all seemed well.

It soon wasn't.

Through the early months of 1943, my mother began to suffer severe headaches. In those days, people didn't go to the doctor, so she was just given a few homeopathic remedies. Nobody knew what was wrong with her and, in April, she died.

I was only five, my sister was ten months old, and my father was left alone: we were all devastated. Unfortunately, there are no photographs of my mother still in existence but even now, more than 60 years later, if I shut my eyes, I can see her face clearly and vividly in my mind's eye.

In mourning, the family rallied round. We all lived within a few hundred metres of each other in the Barracks and, while my infant sister was taken in by my maternal grandparents, it was arranged that I would be brought up by my father with the eager support of six doting aunts.

"Boya," one of my aunts would say, coining the nickname affectionately used by my close relatives. "Please come and eat with us tonight."

"Yes, Artha," I would reply, using the respectful word for aunt in Tamil-Telugu, which was the primary language of the Barracks – I didn't start speaking English until I was six years old.

"Boya, have you finished your homework?"

"No, Artha."

"Boya, you need new shoes."

"Yes, Artha."

"Boya, don't disappoint your father."

"No, Artha."

As the only son of an only son, in the Indian tradition, I was showered with attention and privileges, the more so because I had lost my mother at an early age. I missed her terribly and, out of necessity, learned to look after myself and not rely on anyone else. Maybe this was a silver lining to a dark cloud: a capacity to be independent would serve me well in years to come.

Through my childhood, revering my father and shuffling from aunt to aunt, often feeling uncertain of where I belonged, suffering sporadic instability, Magazine Barracks was my universe.

Named after a large ammunition storage facility nearby, the Barracks was established in 1867 and grew to accommodate 2 500 municipality employees and their families. The settlement became a true microcosm of Indian society, contrasting rich culture and genuine community spirit with material poverty.

The people were oppressed – the white authorities ignored incessant pleas for improved facilities – but, even in helplessness, we were brought up to make the best of life.

Seventy percent of the residents lived in bleak rows of long buildings built from wood and iron, with living quarters on one side of an uneven road and kitchen areas on the other. Life was hard: tin roofs made the Barracks intensely hot in summer and horribly cold in winter.

There was no electricity supply in these areas and, for light and warmth, each family had to make do with the small ration of paraffin collected by each household on a Sunday morning.

We were extremely fortunate to be among the 30 percent of residents who lived in small brick buildings with electricity and, for some households, running water, but with no separate toilet facilities. This status derived from the fact that, many years earlier, after serving his indenture period working in the sugar cane fields, my grandfather had been given a place in this better quality accommodation as soon as he started work as a labourer for the Durban Corporation, and his family had retained the privilege ever since.

The entire Barracks fell under the authority of a supervisor, who had his own house on the perimeter and was more often than not the only white person in the neighbourhood. He was responsible for almost everything, from keeping the streets clean to maintaining law and order with a band of security officers who were employed by the municipality. They were Indian people drawn from our own community, and we called them sirdars.

As I recall, they didn't have a difficult job because crime was rare.

People in the Barracks tended to be religious, with a large Hindu majority and small Christian and Muslim groups, and, as we always liked to say, no beggar's call went unanswered and no collection box went empty in our streets.

Since my family were Hindu, we looked forward to the major festivals, like Deepavali, the festival of lights, and Kavadi and Parthasi, when the Barracks came alive with celebrations.

When I was 14 years old, my father remarried, and converted to Christianity, since his new wife was Christian, but I decided to stay with one aunt or the other and to remain Hindu. Today, I continue to pursue the traditional goals of purity of life, peace and happiness.

There were no shops inside our Barracks, which meant the grocery store down the road did a roaring trade. There were no schools either. However, the Temple Girls' School was not too far away, and, every morning, the boys were dispatched on the 15-minute walk to the Depot Road School.

My closest friends on this daily trek were Bobby Naidoo, an excellent all-round sportsman (now retired in Dallas, Texas), and the late Kotia Naidoo. The three of us grew up together, matriculated together and, give or take a few breaks now and then, kept in touch throughout our lives.

My father never left me in any doubt about the importance of working hard at school. Personal experience taught him the value of literacy, and he was determined I should enjoy the same benefits. First, he took upon himself the task of teaching me the alphabet and, in later years, he never failed to bring home a copy of the *Daily News* and, every evening, he encouraged me to pore over the headlines and the news stories.

"Boya," my aunt Chinamma Parvathy used to ask, "why do you always start with the sports pages?"

"I'm just checking the results, Artha," I would reply.

"There's more to life than sport."

"Yes, Artha," I would say, although I wasn't so sure.

Magazine Barracks was renowned as a hub of sporting activity and, from an early age, I was positively determined to devote every spare minute of my time to some kind, in fact, any kind, of sport; but if I was ever given a choice, through my early teenage years, it would always be soccer.

We used to kick a ball around on a patch of wasteland between school and the Barracks, and local African boys would sometimes join us in these impromptu matches that lasted from after last class at school until sunset.

For us, the colour of our skins was irrelevant. Unfortunately, the ruling National Party government took a very different view, and legislation meant that, at club and national level, soccer was played in four separate structures: the whites had their own league, so did Coloureds, so did blacks and so did we, the Indians.

Only whites were allowed to play international matches, so the 'white' national team was formally recognised by FIFA as 'South Africa'; and the 'Coloured' national team, the 'black' national team and the 'Indian' national team were left to play friendly fixtures against each other.

All our local clubs were affiliated to the South African Indian Football Association and, in this time of contrived racial barriers, we were content to celebrate our heroes playing in the local Indian leagues around Durban. Chappie Kistan, Lighty Chinniah and Siva Millar were stars, and I used to admire Rajgopaul and his brother, nicknamed Matambu.

Our horizons were piteously narrow, but we didn't worry about what we didn't know. As far as I was concerned, at the age of 12, there was no finer player in the world than Matambu.

Then, each October, our soccer fields would be turned into cricket grounds, and we would play on a quick-matting wicket, laid out on compact clay. I remember seeing members of our local cricket club mowing the outfield. In my view, cricket was OK, but it wasn't soccer.

One afternoon in 1949, my friends and I decided to take a stroll down the road to the Kingsmead cricket stadium. We were all aware that the Australian cricket team was touring South Africa at the time and, even though we always felt somewhat detached from matches involving whites-only Springbok teams, somebody said we should go and watch the touring side in the nets.

To our surprise, the Australians seemed quite pleased to see us. The captain, Lindsay Hassett walked over and asked if we would like to bowl at the batsmen. We were cocky enough to accept his offer, and the great Keith Miller was soon taking guard against my hitherto unappreciated off-breaks.

It was fun, and we even went to watch the Australians play a few days later but, in general, we were not bothered about official, whites-only sport. It was hard to show much interest in an institution that showed absolutely no interest in us. Given a choice, we would probably have supported any touring side against the white South African team, but I believe it would be an exaggeration to say we were strongly opposed. We were not that interested.

My favourite summer sport was athletics. Once again, even at school level, the whites kept their own structures and events, but every season, the best Indian, Coloured and black athletes in the country would be assembled for what amounted to the 'non-white' provincial high schools athletics championships.

In 1953, I was selected for the 'non-white' Natal under-16 team to compete at an interprovincial meeting in Paarl, near Cape Town. This was my first trip outside Durban and, as we clambered into an old minibus for the 18-hour drive, I recall feeling as though we were travelling to the other end of the earth.

My event was the 100-yard sprint and, running barefoot on a grass track, I managed to post a hand-held time of 11,3 seconds. It was OK. My friends looked pleased, and I was happy.

Several years later, after leaving school, my sporting interests diversified to swimming. We lived a 20-minute walk from the Indian Ocean, so I joined a local life-saving club and volunteered to become one of the lifeguards who worked weekends at the so-called Indian beach.

Like everything else, Durban's beaches were divided on racial lines, and our task was to keep watch over the people swimming at the beach reserved for Indians. I enjoyed the job.

Every now and then, after finishing a shift, my friends and I used to wander down to the beaches marked as 'Whites Only'; and we would bridle as we passed the hated signs.

"Heh, look over here! Do you remember when the notices on these benches said 'Europeans Only'?"

"Yep."

"You know why they were changed to 'Whites Only'?"

"No."

"Well, the American visitors didn't know where to sit!"

We would laugh. It was funny, and true.

"Seriously, you know why the benches are only for whites?"

"Why?"

"Well, the government has realised that, as black people, we are physically strong enough to stand."

We would laugh again, because laughter and sarcasm seemed like the easiest response to the daily reality that we were classified as second-class citizens in our own country.

The National Party stormed to power in 1948, when I was 10 years old, and their immediate proposition to the Indian community was go back home to the sub-continent, and they would pay the ship's fare. Some accepted the offer of repatriation – after all, Nehru had become Prime Minister in 1947 and India's future seemed bright – but most people preferred to stay because their family roots had grown deep into African soil.

It didn't matter if we were persecuted, deprived, sidelined and disenfranchised, we would stay in South Africa.

It didn't matter if we weren't even allowed to become citizens of the country where we lived, we would stay.

It didn't matter if we were banned from living in the Orange Free State, or if we had to queue at the Indian Immigration Section for a permit to visit Johannesburg, we would stay.

It didn't matter if every public toilet was reserved for whites, which meant desperate young Indians and Africans were mocked as dirty when they could only urinate in the gutters, we would stay.

Apartheid caused offence every single day.

We were classified and ruled. Whites were always on the top rank; Coloured people and Indians came next, and Africans were defined as the dregs of society.

We were divided and ruled. An important element of the National Party government strategy was to sow conflict and hatred between racial groups. Indians were deliberately encouraged to regard Blacks as dangerous and lazy, and Blacks were subtly indoctrinated to think Indians were dishonest and not to be trusted.

On a few occasions, the policy worked. I remember a weekend in 1949 when several thousand incensed blacks ransacked Indian-owned shops in Durban, causing havoc in an Indian settlement called Cato Manor, but, in Natal at least, the Indian and black communities soon reached an understanding that they were both on the same side of the offence.

Political partnerships were established and, at our level, there was no friction when we played soccer with local black boys. Before long, my friends and I were speaking passable Zulu.

Naturally, we were acutely aware that apartheid inflicted very much more trauma and humiliation on black people than it did on us; however, in and around Magazine Barracks, everyday relations between Indians and Blacks were cordial.

As time passed, and such complex issues played on my mind, I started to contemplate the basic paradox standing at the heart of our existence as an Indian community in South Africa.

On the one hand, we were Indians, committed to protecting and sustaining our cultural and religious identity. We felt a natural sense of affinity with India, a loyalty that was affirmed when, after the introduction of apartheid, the New Delhi government was one of the first to impose trade sanctions on South Africa.

In 1950, an official delegation from India visited South Africa and, after meeting the government in Cape Town, the leader of the group, Pandit Kunzru, took the trouble to visit Durban, where he knew most of the Indian population was settled. I was a boy scout at that time, and our particular scout group was selected to welcome Mr Kunzru at a welcome function.

Even though I was only 12, I recall being aware that this man had come all the way from India, that he was on our side, and that he wanted to improve our living conditions.

I also remember how my grandfather regaled me with stories of Mahatma Gandhi, telling how the young lawyer led campaigns of passive resistance against racial discrimination during the 21 years he lived in South Africa, from 1893 until 1914, and how he and his friends had shaved their heads as a sign of protest.

This was our history, our culture and our heritage, and we felt tremendously proud of our Indian origins.

However, on the other hand, we were also eager to be South Africans because we were committed to the country.

This apparent contradiction may have been shared with every immigrant community in every land, but they have caused endless discussions within our community over the years.

Do we belong, or don't we belong? Where is home? Are we Indians or South Africans? Are we Indian South Africans or should we call ourselves South African Indians? Questions of identity and terminology have rumbled through the generations.

The policies of the National Party government did not allow us to settle upon a conclusive answer – the last thing they wanted was even more non-white people feeling like true South Africans – and, for me, personally, the issue remained hazily unresolved until the inauguration of Nelson Mandela as the first President of a fully democratic South Africa in 1994. I was privileged to be involved in the organisation of the event, and I recall being impressed by the motto of the day: Many Cultures, One Nation.

Those four words conveyed the message that there is no conflict between wanting to preserve an Indian culture and being a completely committed South African. Today, I consider myself to be a South African of Indian origin, a member of a defined culture co-existing and uniting with many other groups to make one united nation, the Republic of South Africa.

The phrase 'Strength in Diversity' might be a well-worn cliché, but it rang true in 1994 and has done so ever since.

I daresay it would not have meant much to the Supervisor of Magazine Barracks. He would probably not have understood the concept because, like millions of others in that era, he had been indoctrinated to believe a one-man, one-vote democracy would be a disaster and that blacks were inferior.

My friends and I faced such views every day of our lives, and many of us became politically aware from an early age.

There was a town crier in the Barracks, and he would walk up and down the rutted roads early in the morning, ringing a bell and shouting announcements about the funeral arrangements for someone who had died, or details of a cultural gathering.

"There's a meeting at Red Square," this walking newspaper would bellow, "two o'clock, Sunday afternoon."

From when I was as young as six years old, I understood that such an announcement meant my father was going to put me on his shoulders and carry me to Red Square, a patch of ground in Durban where the South African Indian Congress held its meetings.

My father was a man of strong convictions, and a member of DIMES, the Durban Indian Municipal Employees Society, a well-organised and well-connected trade union that sprung from Magazine Barracks and became respected across the country. Many of its patrons and leaders were well-known, accepted figures in the Congress at both national and provincial level.

So, when the appointed Sunday came, people would steadily make their way to Red Square, or Nichol Square as it was properly named. The nickname 'Red Square' seems to have derived from the fact that people who attended meetings there were generally called 'Communists' or 'Reds' – in those days, of course, almost everybody who opposed apartheid was branded a communist.

And we would stand in the sun and listen to the orators of our community deliver carefully worded speeches.

In the early years, I had no idea what was going on. Perched on my father's shoulders, gazing across a sea of heads and hats, I was literally there for the ride but, into my teens, I took more interest in what was said.

Even now, I have a very clear memory of hearing Dr Mogambery Naicker speak at Red Square. The leader of the Indian community in Durban, he used to wear a small 'Nehru' cap and greet his audience in Tamil before delivering his speech in English, to be understood by Tamil, Hindi, Telugu and Gujarati speakers alike.

He would stand on the back of a lorry, and talk about the poor living conditions of Indian people; he would highlight the laws that made our lives difficult. Dr Naicker would speak for us and yet, with two or three uniformed South African policemen standing nearby, noting what was being said, he would not launch a direct attack on the National Party government.

Like other speakers, he had to speak in a kind of code, which his audience understood, referring obliquely to 'the oppressor', 'the oppressed' and 'current government policy'.

Dr Yusuf Dadoo was another impressive speaker, and he used to travel from Johannesburg to attend meetings. There was also a rousing lady named Dr Goonam, and a man named George Singh. My father used to tell me how he had once taken me to hear the celebrated activist, Braam Fischer, speaking at Red Square.

The South African Indian Congress, the Natal Indian Congress and

DIMES: these were the structures and vehicles for our political activity. Every once in a while, we would hear how people had been woken by a knock on the door in the middle of the night and taken to police stations for interrogation, but this was the price that many individuals were prepared to pay for the cause.

My awareness of these issues increased when I moved on from Depot Road Primary School, and enrolled at Sastri College. Political discussion was common, and the teachers were prepared to be more pointed in the advice they offered about the direction we should be taking in our lives.

They still had to be cautious because, in those days, teachers were regarded as civil servants, employees of the state, and were expressly forbidden from indulging in political debate. However, it was not difficult to read between the lines of what they said in the classroom, and the seeds of activism were sown.

Our teachers encouraged us to think our own thoughts and to conceive our own actions. They gave us the confidence and courage to question the status quo and to challenge authority. They did not advocate or implore. They simply presented the facts and gave us the opportunity to reach our own conclusions.

I was 15 years old, physically small and quiet by nature, not exactly a threat to the government, and yet my teachers inspired me to do something. I wanted to get involved.

The Guardian was a left-wing newspaper usually to be found in our house. My father brought it home every week and, although I didn't much like it when I was a youngster, because it didn't have many photographs, I gradually grew to appreciate its dense columns of liberation news.

There were not many *Guardian* readers in our Barracks, not for any lack of political commitment, but because general levels of literacy were low. However, the publishers wanted to increase the circulation and, when they asked for volunteers to distribute their newspaper through the streets and buildings where I lived, I stepped forward to make a tiny contribution.

The Guardian was eventually banned by the government, but the paper was saved and relaunched as the *New Age*. That was also closed, and a liberal torch was briefly extinguished.

Not every member of the Indian community shared the views expressed at Red Square; and a small but wealthy group founded the South African Indian Organisation, which actively promoted a case for cooperation with the apartheid government.

We called them collaborators, and this organisation received zero support from the working people in our Barracks.

As time passed, and I neared the end of my time at college, my father grew increasingly eager that I should settle upon a career and decide exactly what I wanted to do with my life.

I listened carefully and respectfully but, by this time, I was spending most of my time with my aunts and my sister. There was no animosity between us, but my father had essentially created a new life with his new family, his second wife, my two stepbrothers, Joe and Eric, and my stepsister, Gladys, and, as very often happens in this type of situation, some distance had grown between us.

Nonetheless, I saw my father on a regular basis, and he had made a fair point: I should decide what to do with my life.

As a child, I had dreamed of becoming an aeroplane pilot (or an 'airplane driver' as I thought they were called, until an older friend put me right), because every morning, shortly after seven o'clock, a Dakota passenger jet flew past my bedroom window, and I worshipped the men who flew these machines.

Magazine Barracks was situated directly on the flight path at Stamford Hill, the old Durban airport, and, day after day, I used to wake and hope the red-eye flight to Johannesburg would knock the chimney off our roof as it passed overhead.

"I want to fly a plane like that," I would tell my father, and he was kind enough to let me enjoy the dream rather than disclose the fact that, then, such jobs were reserved for whites.

The reality check eventually happened, and I shifted my goal to making the most of my literacy, and becoming a lawyer or a doctor. Law and medicine were two of very few professions that, in those days, were open to non-whites, and I imagined I would be able to make progress because I had worked hard at school and passed my exams with distinction.

I was wrong. I was told applicants for these professions needed to attend higher education and, unfortunately, we were not able to afford the fees being charged by universities. I tried to sign up for a correspondence course at UNISA, but that didn't work.

Every dream died. I stood by and waved goodbye to school friends, who had achieved worse marks than me but were going to university because their families could pay the fees.

After some reflection, I settled on teaching as a career and secured a place at the Springfield Teacher Training College.

When I wasn't studying, I was playing. When I wasn't playing, I was coaching. Track and field, swimming and soccer were my top sports and, week after week, I dedicated myself to being the best I could be, seeking every available piece of knowledge.

I became involved in clubs, took responsibility for teams in all three sports and taught at several schools in Natal.

However, by the mid-1960s, it had become clear to me that I would have to travel overseas to reach my potential. There were not enough opportunities for 'non-white' coaches in racist South African sports structures catering exclusively for whites.

The general political temperature had also started to rise and, in our community, we could feel the heat generated by the Treason Trials, the Sharpeville massacre and other outrages. One day, when many Indians were arrested and thrown into jail, I remember being told to put my pocket money, just a few pennies, into a collection box that was being passed round to help the affected families.

My professional frustration, exacerbated by a sense that the general situation inside South Africa was deteriorating, inspired me to investigate opportunities in other countries.

"You have everything you need here," my sister insisted when I first raised the possibility of studying in England.

"That's the problem," I replied. "I don't. I want to be the best coach possible. I want to learn from the latest research, and I don't have access to that kind of opportunity here."

The obstacle, as ever, was money. It was going to cost me £87 to travel to England by boat, and the British authorities would only allow me into the country if I arrived with £100 in cash. The situation was simple: if I could find £187, I would be able to continue my education in England.

My hopes were pinned on the Natal Indian Teachers Society, an organisation that was prepared to lend money to young teachers as long as the funds were to be used in such a way that they would represent an investment in their skills and their future.

Discussions continued, and we reached agreement when I decided to cede my pension rights to the society in return for an advance of £100. I am not sure whether this was a great deal, but I was determined to make the trip.

My family seemed concerned by my impending departure, but they understood the strength of my ambition and appeared pleased that I was starting to realise some of my goals.

"What will you do when you arrive?" my sister asked.

"I'm not sure," I said, "but I have people to call and I'm sure I will find work as a teacher and find a course."

"How can you be sure?"

"I'll be fine, I promise."

So, on September 1st, 1966, somehow keeping myself together, I packed my suitcase and said goodbye to friends and family. As we drove away towards the docks, where I would board the ship, I recall looking out of the window towards Magazine Barracks, my home for my formative years.

I would not have that privilege again because the Durban City Council had taken a decision that this Indian settlement was located in an area of the city that, under the terms of the Group Areas Act, would henceforth be reserved for white people. So, the residents, including many members of my family, suffered the indignity of being forcibly removed to Chatsworth, 20 kilometres away.

With the stroke of a mercilessly careless official pen, many thousands of innocent lives were hurled into chaos and confusion, and an entire established community was shovelled to a barren place devoid of shops, schools, hospitals and sports fields.

Many people found their new travel costs unaffordable; most found their new lives miserable and intolerable.

Our Barracks was bulldozed to extinction, but the spirit of the place remains among those of us who lived there.

WIDE WORLD

The Captain heard first, but the news quickly spread through the ship. Hendrik Verwoerd, the Prime Minister of South Africa, the man renowned as the architect of apartheid, had been assassinated at Parliament in Cape Town. I could hardly believe it.

Most of the passengers on our voyage from South Africa to England were white South Africans and they began to gather in small groups around the ship, looking stunned and sad.

One agitated lady, whom I had briefly met during dinner the previous evening, approached me and asked if I had heard the news. "It's appalling," she said. "So tragic, isn't it?"

I nodded awkwardly, and hurried on. As an apprehensive young teacher heading overseas for the first time, this was neither the time nor the place to expose my political convictions.

However, later that night, I found myself sitting with a group of young Australians and it soon became clear I was among kindred spirits. "Well, if you ask me, this is the best thing that could have happened to South Africa," one said. "Let's just hope they get someone more progressive now."

With that, he asked me if I wanted a drink. Verwoerd's death was hardly a victory because nobody believed his policies would be buried with him, but I was not inclined to mourn his passing either.

"I'll have a beer please," I replied.

For me, the atmosphere aboard the ship was stimulating and liberating and, as we ploughed north through the grey Atlantic, I continued to meet a wide variety of interesting people from different backgrounds, an amazing number of whom would cross my path many times in years to come.

There was a journalist called Ian Hobbs. He became the London correspondent for South African Associated Newspapers, later Times Media Ltd, and was especially helpful during the years when I worked for the South African Non-Racial Olympic Committee (SANROC) in England.

There was also a young woman who had been detained in South Africa. She had been beaten up by a security officer who held her hair and beat her head on the floor until she was unconscious, bruising her so much that, she told a friend, her blackened eyes extended to her chin. Her name was Stephanie Kemp, and she was on her way to London to join a brilliant young lawyer called Albie Sachs, whom she later married.

Joining the ship when we docked in Cape Town before heading up the west coast of Africa was an elegant woman named May Brutus, together with her three children. They were on their way to join her husband who, she said, was planning to board the ship in the Canary Islands.

"Is your husband called Dennis?" I asked.

"That's right," she smiled.

Dennis Brutus was well known in political circles. Trained as a teacher in Port Elizabeth, he had emerged as a determined and charismatic leader in the nonracial sports movement, operating beyond the control of the establishment. When others tended to talk, Dennis acted.

He was primarily responsible for the formation of SANROC inside the country and, during the course of the early 1960s, was variously arrested, imprisoned on Robben Island and shot when trying to escape from the police. He managed to leave for England at the end of 1965, and now his wife and children were joining him there.

The days passed slowly, as I eagerly anticipated Dennis's arrival. He duly boarded the ship in Tenerife, as planned, and soon afterwards, I plucked up the courage to introduce myself. Nervously I explained my background in Durban and my plans to study physical education in England.

He listened carefully and proved extraordinarily affable. It turned out that we had many mutual friends and we seemed to get along, talking for hours as the ship churned on towards Europe.

Dennis told me how he had decided to reform SANROC as a nonracial sports organisation in London, and I said I would be very keen to do whatever I could to help the cause.

"That's fine, Samba, but be careful," he told me. "Always remember you are going back to South Africa, so be careful who you mix with in London. You must be discreet because there are spies everywhere. If they identify you as an activist, your life will be difficult when you get home."

"I understand," I replied, grateful for the advice.

"If you come to a SANROC meeting, you will be listed as a visitor from South Africa, but not named."

"OK," I said, "but I would still like to help."

Dennis gave me his telephone number, and, as soon as I was settled in England, I contacted him and began to get better acquainted with SANROC, and its activities in London.

With hindsight, the coincidence that such a prominent figure in the anti-apartheid sports movement should have happened to be travelling on the same ship as me had a profound effect on my life. I may still have worked in the same field, but Dennis proved a great inspiration to me.

We would not always agree on everything and, in years to come, relations became strained, but I will never forget the kindness and generosity he showed towards me when we met on the boat.

It was a beautiful autumn day when we finally docked in Southampton, and I vividly remember my sense of genuine excitement as I arrived in England for the first time. I had been to Mozambique for a weekend, and I had spent a few days in Southern Rhodesia, but varying forms of racial discrimination remained in both countries, and this was my first experience of a genuinely free and democratic country.

Just seeing people do and say whatever they liked gave me a sense of walking outside and breathing fresh air after 28 years of being locked in a stale room, existing as a second-class citizen.

I was excited and invigorated, and took the train to London.

My plan was to find a teaching post as quickly as possible, and save enough of my salary to pay the fees for a course at a college of physical education; and my primary contact was the National Union of Teachers (NUT), who, I had been assured, would be helpful and sympathetic to my situation.

So I called their telephone number early on Friday morning, and was told the person I needed would only be back in the office on Monday. Three days of frenetic sightseeing beckoned.

Trafalgar Square, Buckingham Palace, the Tower of London... everything was a blur and, by Sunday, the gloss was beginning to wear thin. I had arrived in London with the same innocence as Dick Whittington, and it had not taken long for me to realise the streets were not, in fact, paved with gold.

England had just won the soccer World Cup and the Beatles were at the top of the charts, flower power and the peace movement were gaining momentum, and the Sixties were 'swinging', but, to me, many buildings looked grim and grey, and much of the housing was dilapidated and run-down. I happened to mention my creeping sense of disappointment to a fellow guest at my hotel, and he said at least the shopping was good.

"I'm not sure," I replied. "I think the shops in Durban are better."

Monday morning dawned and, alone in the city, I needed a break. I arrived at the offices of the NUT as they opened, and was introduced to Mrs Webb, a name I will never forget.

"Can I help you?" she asked, peering over mounds of paper on her desk.

I explained my situation: South African teacher, arrived in England to further my education, less than £100 in my pocket, after paying the cost of my hotel and food over the weekend. I suppose Mrs Webb would have been perfectly entitled to show me the door. Instead, she showed me the future.

"Have you applied to any schools?" she asked.

"I did write some letters from Durban," I told her, "but they all said they would only be able to process my application once I had arrived in England. So, I have nothing arranged at the moment."

She rested her index finger on her chin, thought for a moment, reached for her telephone book and smiled at me. "All right," she said quietly. "I think it's going to be easier for you to find a teaching post in London, rather than outside, and, with a bit of luck, I might have just the thing for you."

I sat in silent hope as Mrs Webb telephoned a primary school in Dagenham, in Essex, east of London, and said she had found the perfect teacher for them. After a while, she put her hand over the receiver and asked me if I would be able to go for an interview at the school on Wednesday morning. I nodded eagerly.

"Well, that's arranged then," she said, putting down the phone. "It's the Richard Alibon School, and the headmaster's name is Sidney Ling. He is expecting you at eleven on Wednesday."

"Thank you very much," I said. "Thank you very, very much."

I believe that, in a very profound sense, Sidney Ling understood me from the moment we met. He had always taken an interest in South African issues and, in every way, he knew where I was coming from and what I wanted to achieve. We met at eleven, and he explained the vacant post. I outlined my qualifications and, during lunch, he asked when I could start.

"What about next week?" I suggested, unable to believe my luck.

"That suits me," the headmaster replied.

So, barely five days after arriving at Southampton with nothing, the kindness of two complete strangers, Mrs Webb and Mr Ling, enabled me to start preparing for a full-time job at a London school.

In fact, my first day didn't go well. My lessons in the morning passed without incident. The school was obviously in a working-class area of the town but the buildings were quite well maintained and the children were cheerful, lively and eager to learn. I presided over lunch without difficulty.

Then, just after half past two in the afternoon, the children returned to my classroom. I was surprised and told them to go home. It was their turn to look surprised, but they quickly dispersed.

By three o'clock, the school telephone was ringing incessantly and annoyed parents were approaching the school gates with confused children in tow. I was asked to see Mr Ling in his office.

"Sam, is it true that you sent your class home at half past two?"

"Yes," I replied, blissfully ignorant.

"OK," the headmaster said, with amazing calm given the bedlam erupting around him. "The only thing is we usually have two lessons in the afternoon, and the children are used to going home at quarter to four."

I was amazed. Wherever I had previously taught in Durban, the school day had ended at 2.30 and, foolishly, I had automatically assumed the same timetable would apply to schools in London.

This embarrassing experience taught me to double-check everything in the school timetable and I managed to avoid any more disasters. My teaching colleagues seemed aware of the situation in South Africa and some of them, like Russell O'Callaghan, became good friends.

Life began to settle into a steady rhythm. I was renting a cheap bedsit near Marble Arch, which meant I had to travel across London every morning and every evening, but the underground was convenient and, 40 years on, I can recall my daily route: Central Line from Lancaster Gate, change at Mile End. In my second year in London, I would board as the lodger of a South African family, who had immigrated.

The nearest football club to school was West Ham United and, at one local school function, I had my picture taken with the club's three great heroes at the time, Bobby Moore, Geoff Hurst and Martin Peters. I went to watch matches at Upton Park, and also at Chelsea, Fulham and the Arsenal, but I generally travelled to White Hart Lane because Jimmy Greaves was my favourite player and I supported Spurs.

In the summer, I enjoyed watching cricket as a paying spectator at Lord's and the Oval, and, oddly enough, I was sitting in the crowd at the Oval Test match in 1968 when Basil D'Oliveira scored his famous 168 and was still not included, initially at least, in the England squad to tour South Africa.

Of course, there were days when I missed my family and friends, and I just missed South Africa, but I immersed myself in school life, coaching the swimming and football teams in addition to teaching, and, above all, I was always able to fall back upon the support and friendship of Sidney Ling.

I am not exactly sure what we had in common. It's true we shared a passion for sport, and we also shared a disciplined approach to life: he had served as RAF ground staff personnel during the Second World War and ran his school in a military fashion. I also preferred everything to be organised.

Perhaps, from the start, we both followed our instincts: he was happy to employ someone he had just met, and I was willing to work in a tough area. He later told me how, in my first few days, he didn't think I would last long in Dagenham. I laughed and told him those were my feelings exactly.

In fact, on both sides, our initial gut feeling stood the test of time, and we became such close friends that, for many years to come, whenever I was in London for Christmas, even after I got married, I would spend the day as a guest in the home of Sidney Ling, his wife Gwen and their two sons.

Now into his nineties, Sidney is long retired but he remains a close friend, someone who still seems to understand me. We communicate regularly and I remain indebted to him.

In the event, I needed to work for two years at the Richard Alibon School before I had saved enough of my salary to afford the fees for a course at a college of physical education. If somebody had told me it would take that long when I first arrived in Southampton, I might have turned around and gone home but, looking back, the two years I spent at Sidney Ling's school unfolded as a very happy period of my life.

My father, Rungan Ramsamy, on the right, served as a member of DIMES, the Durban Indian Municipality Employees Society, and made me politically aware from an early age.

After the early death of my mother, I was looked after by my aunts and uncles. This is my earliest photograph, taken with a sister and brother of my late mother, my aunt Amoy and my uncle Jack.

This was my class at Depot Road School, an Indians-only school in Durban, 1947. I am seated third from the right in the front row.

Football was my favourite sport as a teenager and, in 1954, I played for the Sunrise team in Magazine Barracks. I am standing second from the left in the back row.

We lived close to the beach and I enjoyed swimming. So, as soon as I turned 17, I joined the volunteer lifesaving group that worked each weekend on the 'Indians-only' beach. I am kneeling on the right.

Apartheid engulfed us. My friends and I used to laugh at the whites-only signs, but it was hard to accept official classification as a second-class citizen.

John Rugg was a former professional footballer from Scotland, and he agreed to coach the Natal Indian schools provincial side. My friend Sagren Naidoo, middle row extreme left, and I, middle row extreme right, were happy to serve as his assistants.

Samba Ramsamy to conduct swim clinic

Samba Ramsamy accomplished Sports Coach says that Ellis Brown's delicious flavour trained him to appreciate good coffee.

ELLIS BROWN
10c -⊙- 10c
COFFEE & CHICORY MIXTURE

After studying in England, I returned to Durban in 1969 and began coaching athletics, football and swimming in the nonracial sports structures. This brought me some fame and, right, the occasional endorsement.

I worked and studied in England from 1966 to 1969, and returned to London as an exile in 1972. Within a week of arriving, in both 1966 and 1972, I was lucky enough to get a teaching job at the Richard Alibon School in East London. Sidney Ling, the headmaster, standing in the middle of the back row in this 1967 staff photograph, was a constant source of loyalty and support.

Initially as a volunteer, and then from 1978 as an employee, I became involved in the South African Non-Racial Olympic Committee (SANROC) and its campaign to ensure the total isolation of South African sport, from conference to conference, congress to congress, all around the world.

These are four men united by a cause: Chris de Broglio, left, a former South African weightlifting champion, served as Secretary-General of SANROC for many years; Lamine Diack, second left, was instrumental in securing South Africa's expulsion from the IAAF, the world governing body of athletics, and has now become its President; Andrew Young, former US Ambassador to the United Nations, has always been a great support.

My involvement with SANROC created an opportunity for me to spend a year studying sports science in Leipzig, East Germany, right, where I met and fell in love with Helga Zimmerman. Helga's parents and sister joined us on our wedding day in 1977, above, but my family in Durban had to be content with photos sent in the post.

The communist East German sports structure has been broadly criticised, and there were certainly abuses, but I found much to admire. This swimming coaches' course in Leipzig was stimulating and well structured.

Syed Wajid Ali delivered a memorably powerful speech at the IAAF Congress in 1976, supporting the motion to expel South Africa. I told the respected Pakistani sports official that he had 'steamrollered' the opposition.

Ydnekatcheou Tessema, of Ethiopia, was a founding member of the Confederation of African Football and always stood firm in the front line of the fight against apartheid in sport. He proved a notably astute tactician in the administrative corridors of international sport.

Abraham Ordia, of Nigeria, centre, was another stalwart of our campaign. He was an extremely influential leader from an extremely influential country. Enuga Reddy, of India, left, served as Head of the United Nations Centre Against Apartheid and proved a wonderful ally, particularly in establishing the UN Register of Sports Contacts with South Africa.

Jeremy Pope worked at the Commonwealth Secretariat but also emerged as a hero of the SANROC cause, particularly in drafting legal documents and devising strategy.

Jean-Claude Ganga, seated in the centre, emerged as one of the most vocal and eloquent supporters of our cause. Here, the IOC member from the Congo is in full flow, explaining his proposal for the timetable for achieving unity in South African sport. Lamine Diack, now President of the International Association of Athletic Federations (IAAF), is standing behind him, and Ismail Bhamjee, of Botswana, later a Fédération Internationale de Football Association (FIFA) Executive Committee member, is standing directly behind me.

Politically, I was mindful of Dennis Brutus's advice on the boat. Every now and then, I did visit the ANC office run by Reg September, and I did attend an Anti-Apartheid Movement meeting in a committee room at the Houses of Parliament but, by and large, I was very cautious. As Dennis had warned, there were South African government spies everywhere and I did not want to attract victimisation when I got back to Durban.

The issue of apartheid was alive in London during the late 1960s, but few people understood what was happening in South Africa and it often seemed to be only one item on a long political agenda. People were more interested in discussing Vietnam, student riots in Paris and the peace movement.

I took an active interest in all these matters, but managed always to keep my head down, never to raise my voice and never to be seen at the forefront of any meeting or demonstration. I was eager to make a contribution, and to meet people, but I consistently erred on the side of discretion.

Unseen and unheard, I did want to get involved with SANROC, the nonracial sports organisation founded by Dennis Brutus in South Africa in 1963, then banned by the government and reformed as an international pressure group in London, drawing attention to racial discrimination in South African sport.

Dennis was supported in SANROC by the immense contribution of Chris de Broglio, a former weightlifting champion who had represented South Africa at the 1958 World Championships in Hungary, but had then seen the light and dedicated himself to coaching African and Indian weightlifters in Durban.

His conscience led him into the nonracial sports movement and the wider political struggle and, harassed by the authorities, he used his Mauritian passport and emigrated to London. There, he demonstrated a brain to match his brawn, buying the Portland Court Hotel near Marble Arch, and building a strong business.

Chris offered his time and expertise to SANROC on a purely honorary basis, as everyone did until 1978, and he provided the organisation with its first head office in the basement of his hotel.

Through so many meetings and campaigns over a period of 14 years, through success and disappointments, through tasks great and small, Chris de Broglio wholeheartedly and selflessly committed himself to SANROC and the cause of equality in South African sport. He eventually moved to Mauritius and, today, lives in France, but his enormous contribution will not be forgotten. In hard times, he held the bridge.

I used to appear at the office every now and then, usually at weekends, offering to help out, and we would sit and discuss SANROC projects and the latest news from South Africa. I felt passionate about the cause and privileged to learn from established campaigners like Dennis and Chris.

In September 1968, I was finally able to afford the fees of higher education, and I enrolled in a one-year course in physical and health education at the Carnegie College of Physical Education in Leeds. After two years of enjoying the political and cultural melting pot of London, I was heading to the north of England.

It didn't take very long for me to realise I was the only non-Briton on my course, and one of very few Indians at the college, but I settled quickly and sensed no form of discrimination. I shared a house with four white students and enjoyed an active social life. The course was everything I had hoped for, well constructed, up to date and stimulating, and I enjoyed a positive sense of growing, personally and professionally, day by day.

An important element of the end-of-year exams was a written paper, and I settled upon the subject of 'The Apartheid Polices of the South African Government'. My text was distinguished by a wealth of eyewitness material, supplied by Messrs Brutus and De Broglio, and I duly secured my diploma.

"So, was it worth it?" my sister Devi asked as soon as I arrived home in August 1969.

"Yes, it was," I replied, smiling. "It certainly was."

That night, I dined with my aunt Ambrutham, who had invited me to stay in her house. It was good to be home.

My brand-new qualification from England created a range of teaching opportunities for me in Durban, but I was looking particularly for a position that would give me a decent salary and still allow me the time to pursue my passion for coaching, whether in swimming, soccer or track and field.

I enjoyed working in the classroom, but I had become motivated by the thought of coaching young blacks to a level where they could compete on equal terms with whites. Maybe, in a small way, I could use my hard-earned knowledge to achieve equality in an unequal society.

It wasn't going to be easy. The South African Soccer Federation (SASF) was the strongest nonracial sports body at the time, and Aces United was one of its leading clubs. Several questions were asked when the new coach of Aces United was announced as... Samba Ramsamy. I set to work.

The team was composed of African, Indian and Coloured players, and they all seemed to accept the strategies that I had brought from England. Luckily, in my first season, we kept our supporters happy by winning the Mainstay Cup, the SASF's premier knockout competition.

"Are you eating with us tonight?" my aunt always used to ask.

"Sorry," I would reply. "I'm going to a committee meeting."

Most evenings, every weekend: there was always something else to be done. Aside from my responsibilities as a teacher and soccer coach, I also accepted the positions of both President of the nonracial Natal High Schools Athletics Association and national coach of the nonracial SA Swimming Federation.

I was particularly pleased to be involved in athletics because it meant I was able to contribute to giving the children the same opportunities I had at their age. But, as the months passed, I began devoting more and more time to swimming, eagerly disproving the racist lie that blacks cannot swim.

My services were also required in the boardroom. In 1970, the non-racial SA Swimming Federation wrote a series of letters to the all-white South African Swimming Union (SASU), persistently requesting a meeting to discuss the formation of a unified swimming body. We received no response at first but, eventually, a meeting was arranged.

I was appointed to lead our delegation and, aware that SASU was dominated by relatively enlightened English speakers, we initially felt reasonably optimistic. Both sides affirmed their desire to unite and administer the sport as one. This was promising.

"The principle of merit selection is important," said Roy Clegg, the SASU president. "We strongly believe the best swimmers must always be chosen to represent South Africa in international events."

"Agreed," we replied.

This response prompted some members of our delegation to take a sharp intake of breath, but we didn't want to waste time arguing this issue, even though we realised it meant our swimmers would probably not have a chance to swim at international level. We wanted to see how far SASU was prepared to go.

I continued: "For us, the principle of open participation is most important. Every South African must have a fair and equal opportunity to swim, and they must be allowed to swim together, from the highest level down to the grass roots."

In blunt terms, we were demanding the end of segregation in swimming, nothing more, and nothing less.

The SASU delegation listened and nodded, and said they would have to consult with the government before reverting to us with their position. We didn't hold our breath, and were not surprised when, some weeks later, we were informed by SASU that the government had refused to change their policy of segregation in sport, and SASU was bound to uphold the law.

Our process had reached a dead end, but the white swimming establishment should at least be credited with an attempt to reach across the racial divide. In contrast, the deeply conservative athletics and cycling bodies refused even to recognise, let alone meet, their nonracial counterparts.

There were other isolated attempts to make progress.

Marshall Lee, a bright journalist with the *Rand Daily Mail*, facilitated a private match between Jasmat Dhiraj, the leading 'non-white' tennis player of the era, and Cliff Drysdale, the celebrated white South African then ranked No 4 in the world. Drysdale won in two closely contested sets and, when news of the match became public, he declared Dhiraj was good enough to play for South Africa in the forthcoming Davis Cup match against Spain.

The President of the South African Tennis Union responded by saying Drysdale should concentrate on playing the game and leave questions of administration and selection to the officials.

Another brave voice had been raised, and another official door had been slammed shut. Every liberal idea, every unification initiative unavoidably collided against the brick wall of intransigent apartheid doctrine, and was promptly shattered.

Now and then, almost comically, multiracial sport took place under the noses of the government. A series of Coloured footballers managed to play in the 'white' professional league by westernising their names and concealing their race. Archie Christopher excelled for Rangers and Smiley Moosa called himself Smiley Williams and played for Arcadia Shepherds until questions were asked and he was expelled from the league.

Well-meaning people on both sides tried to find middle ground, but any fond hope that sport could somehow inspire and lead a wider process of racial integration was firmly crushed.

Perhaps carried away by optimism, I had believed some kind of unity was possible, especially in swimming, but reality dawned and I decided to concentrate more of my time on coaching.

One warm evening, a close friend and activist, Rajendra Chetty, contacted me at home with an unusual proposal.

"Sam," he said. "You know Ellis Brown coffee?"

"Sure," I replied.

"Well, the distributors want you to endorse their coffee in a series of newspaper advertisements."

"OK," I said, unsure of whether he was joking.

"And they are willing to pay you a fixed sum every time the advertisement appears in the newspaper."

The deal was done, and the ads featuring me drinking Ellis Brown coffee started to appear in print. I received my pittance, which seemed scant compensation for the fact that my friends began to tease me relentlessly. My coaching efforts appeared to have given me some kind of public profile in the African, Indian and Coloured communities around Durban, even though I doubted whether anyone cared which coffee I preferred.

In an ideal world, I would have filled my days with coaching, enjoying sport in its purest form, but apartheid South Africa was far from an ideal world. Whether we liked it or not, it was impossible to be involved in non-racial sport and somehow to remain blissfully removed from political issues.

"Keep politics out of sport," white South Africans would often proclaim, incredibly oblivious to the fact that it was the white government that had ruthlessly imposed their political system on sport.

As Africans, Coloureds and Indians, we could not so easily ignore the reality. Apartheid determined where and with whom we could play. Apartheid denied us basic facilities and coaching. Apartheid even prevented us from playing for our country at international level; still, we were supposed to keep politics out of sport! So, I continued to attend meetings, and take an interest in the political sports agenda.

During one such informal gathering, at the home of a friend in Chatsworth, the conversation had drifted to a problem initially identified by Chris de Broglio in London, specifically that, ever since SANROC was forced overseas, there had been no macro-sports, umbrella body for 'non-white' sport in South Africa.

This vacuum enabled the establishment 'white' Olympic Committee to gain credibility by projecting itself to the international community as South Africa's only macro-sports body. That night in Chatsworth, everyone accepted the need for a new organisation to oversee the nonracial sport codes.

I discussed the concept with Farouk Khan, a journalist in Durban, who still works for the *Daily News* today, and with MN Pather, then Secretary of the SA Non-Racial Lawn Tennis Association; together, we developed a strategy and canvassed support from the nonracial sports movement. We were sowing the seeds of the South African Council on Sport (SACOS), a body destined to play a major role in the evolution of a national sports structure.

We eventually arranged a round-table conference, which I attended as a member of the delegation from the swimming federation, and an ad hoc committee was formed to advance the process. MN Pather was appointed as Secretary of the committee, and Norman Middleton, then the President of the South African Soccer Federation, was elected as Chairman.

Out of this committee, in 1973, emerged SACOS.

As the months passed, almost imperceptibly, and certainly without any clear proof, I was starting to sense the authorities were taking an unhealthy interest in my words and deeds. At times, I felt sure I was being watched and maybe even followed. Other times, I shook my head and thought I was being paranoid. At the very least, however, I had learned to take care.

Only the previous year, in 1970, the day after the IOC had formally withdrawn its recognition of South Africa, I had stepped perilously close to the edge of trouble during a visit by the provincial Inspector of Physical Education to the school in Durban where I was teaching.

"So, Mr Ramsamy, I assume you have heard the news from the IOC," the Inspector asked pointedly when he arrived in my classroom, followed by an unidentified man in light grey clothes and light grey shoes.

"Yes," I replied, trying to disguise a hangover.

In truth, the previous night, my friends and I had been celebrating the IOC's decision with enthusiasm and more alcohol than we had consumed in the previous 12 months.

"It's a sad day for South Africa, isn't it?" the inspector persisted.

An honest answer – that it was actually a fantastic day – would have got me fired on the spot, finishing my career as a teacher and seriously jeopardising my future as a coach.

So I swallowed hard and replied: "Yes, it is rather sad."

The following day, an Afrikaans newspaper printed a story that quoted 'an Indian teacher' as saying the IOC decision was 'very sad'. The man in grey shoes had been a journalist but, mercifully, he had not named me in his article. At that time, I was unknown among whites.

It had been a lucky escape. Like so many people, I was living on a tightrope. If I had answered truthfully, I would have lost my job. Instead, I had pretended, and almost lost my reputation.

So, I became wary of talking politics with anyone outside my close circle of friends: I trusted Percy Reddy, a colleague who had been taken in for questioning by the Special Branch, and I confided in the late Morgan Naidoo, a journalist who became involved in swimming, later became a stalwart and President of SACOS, and eventually became a 'banned person'.

Scarcely anybody else received the benefit of my doubt. I believed that, as long as I was broadly perceived as a coach involved in sport, the authorities would leave me alone.

Every now and then, I couldn't help myself.

Early in 1971, I accepted a position as a seconded lecturer at the Springfield College of Education, the institution where I had studied 14 years previously. It suited me because I was able to maintain my coaching commitments and I enjoyed the opportunity to work with older students.

"Mr Ramsamy," one of them asked, "what do you think about the Republic Celebration Games?"

I paused, considering the loaded question.

The Games were structured along racial lines, with separate events for the separate races, and were being organised to mark the 10th anniversary of the founding of the Republic.

"Well, I'm not sure," I replied, guardedly.

In fact, I was well aware that the entire nonracial sports movement had not only decided to take no part in these Games but was planning to stage demonstrations against the event. The same young man persisted: "Mr Ramsamy, do you think we should boycott the Games?"

I looked at him carefully, and somehow seemed to recognise the same kind of resolution and anger that had characterised my own youth. "Well," I replied, "that is an option."

Through the weeks that followed, I helped to organise what turned out to be an extremely effective student sabotage of the Games.

Towards the end of 1971, I was encouraged to apply for a vacant position of full-time lecturer at Springfield. Most of the senior staff at the College were white, even though all the students were Indian and Coloured, but my Head of Department, Adrian Liversage, said I was best qualified for the job and made a personal recommendation on my behalf. Everyone knew that, in his long tenure, his advice had never been overruled.

Someone else got the job. Most people were surprised, but Mr Liversage was so amazed that he arranged to visit the Indian Education Department and find out what had happened. He returned to Springfield the same Friday and called me to a meeting that would change the course of my life.

"Sam, how are you?" he asked, kindly.

"I'm fine," I replied, sensing his disappointment was much greater than mine. I had wanted the security of a full-time job, but it was far from the most important ambition in my life.

Adrian Liversage was a soft-spoken man, generally to be found sitting on his own, content with his own company. He and I had never discussed politics but, somehow, in his facial expressions and gestures, I sensed he was sympathetic to the suffering of people who were not white. I liked him.

"Sam," he continued, in hushed and deliberate tones, "I need to tell you two things. Firstly, my doctor says I am suffering from cancer. He has no idea how long I have to live, but it may not be long."

"I'm sorry," I said.

"It's all right but, please Sam, I want to tell you something else, but I do need you to promise you will keep it secret until after I am dead. I am sorry to ask you this, but it's very important."

"OK, I promise."

"Well, Sam," he continued, barely whispering now, "you are under investigation by the Special Branch, and the only reason you did not get the full-time position was the authorities believe you were heavily involved in the campaign to sabotage the Republic Celebration Games earlier this year.

"I don't think they have very much evidence against you at the moment, but they certainly seem to think they will get to you before long.

"This is my advice: quietly resign; tell everyone you are upset about being overlooked for the post, and that you want to go back to England and continue your studies or even try something else. There is no time to lose, so make plans. Get out of the country without a fuss, while you still can."

Walking home, I felt numb, bewildered, confused. What should I do? How should I react? What would I tell my friends and family? I couldn't tell them anything. I had promised. Through Saturday and Sunday, I must have appeared subdued at home, as I tried to contemplate my next step.

In fact, there were no options. Early on the Monday morning – it was December 13th, 1971, a particularly warm summer's day in Durban, as I recall – I arrived at Springfield and delivered my letter of resignation. I gave the College three months' notice, in terms of my contract, and vaguely indicated that I wanted to leave teaching and move into the field of sports consultancy. I had deliberately decided not to mention anything about planning to go overseas because I didn't want to arouse any unnecessary suspicion.

My life had suddenly become almost surreal. There were moments in the weeks that followed when I almost convinced myself that everything was just a bad dream: that I was not being pursued by the Special Branch, that I did not have to resign, that I would not have to leave home with absolutely no idea when I would return, that I didn't have to lie to my family and friends… that, somehow, I would wake up and be fine.

It didn't happen. As the weeks passed, people became accustomed to the fact that I was leaving Springfield, and moving on. It was not unusual, and my enthusiasm for sport was well known.

However, during January, I slowly started mentioning the possibility of going back to study in England. Most of my family and friends seemed a bit surprised, but not shocked. I had spent time in London before, and come back, and they accepted the idea of going back for another spell abroad.

My father didn't say much. I remember how he sat and listened to my plans, and I clearly recall wondering if he sensed something was suspicious. In any event, he said nothing and gave me his blessing. My sister, Devi, was hurt, much more upset than when I first left home six years before.

"I don't understand why you have to go," she said. "We need you here."

"I want to study again," I said, uncomfortably.

My aunt then asked: "Why can't you study here?"

"I just can't."

They looked into my eyes. Did they see something? Could they tell I wasn't telling them the real reason? Did they know something had happened? To this day, I can't answer these questions.

My closest friends – Bobby Naidoo and Percy Reddy – listened to what I had to say, but they didn't push me to explain. That was the way we talked to each other in those days: if I didn't elaborate, they didn't ask.

Through this almost intolerable period of my life, there were many times when I was talking to my sister, or my aunts and cousins, or with my oldest friends, and I felt an urge to beckon them closer, and tell them the real reason why I had to leave South Africa. At least, they would have known the truth. But, each time, I resisted and kept my promise to Adrian Liversage.

The days slipped away. Some of my friends arranged an upbeat farewell party, where everyone seemed quite jovial. I vividly remember phoning Mr Liversage to say thank you and goodbye; he quietly wished me everything of the best, and said he knew I would do well in whatever I did. On my last night, I arrived at the house of my sister and her husband, Peter Perumal, and enjoyed a typical Indian feast with them.

Then, suddenly, it was March 14th, 1972, and I was standing in the departure lounge at Durban airport, beside two large suitcases packed with my earthly belongings, and an air ticket in my hand.

My sister was crying. I held her, and told her to look after herself. Then I turned towards my father, and my cousin, Asothie, and we shook hands and they told me gently: "Good luck, Samba. We'll miss you."

It was hard, exceptionally hard. I managed to smile, turned and slowly walked towards the departure gate. I looked back one last time, and waved goodbye. I am glad I looked back again because, as my life unfolded, I would not see my sister for another 19 years, and I never saw my father again.

INTO EXILE

My room at Chris de Broglio's hotel in London was not large, but it was clean and comfortable and the SANROC stalwart had kindly offered me a place to stay as soon as I arrived in London. I sat down at the desk and started to write a letter home to my sister, back in Durban…

Portland Court Hotel
Marble Arch
London
March 21st, 1972

Dear Devi,

I hope everything is well. It has only been a week since I left South Africa, but I am already missing my life at home: my job, my friends, my sport, you and the family. There are some things which I will only be able to tell you later, but I feel angry and in despair.

I am angry because I am unable to live peacefully and freely in my own country, and I am in despair because the struggle against apartheid will be long and hard.

Ever since Dad took me to hear the speakers at Red Square, I have been aware of the oppression in South Africa, and I know I was brought up in such a way that I would not simply accept our fate. I am grateful for that, but, sitting alone here in London, facing the consequences of my actions, I can't pretend it is not hard.

Devi, now that I am over here, I want to make a difference and I feel I can do that in sport. There are plenty of people involved in political issues, but sport is my niche.

I have made contact with the people at SANROC, who are campaigning for the total isolation of South African sport. Some people may think sport is relatively trivial, but an international boycott can help our cause because it puts real pressure on the government, and it is a clear and constant expression of global protest.

I think it can work, and I feel committed to SANROC. Dennis Brutus has gone to live in the United States, so Chris de Broglio is pleased to have some help.

Otherwise, everything is fine. I called Sidney Ling on the day I arrived, and, as good as his word, he has arranged a teaching job for me at his school. So, nearly four years after leaving, I am going back to work at the Richard Alibon School east of London tomorrow. Hopefully, I will settle down quickly.

Devi, look after yourself, give my love to all and write soon.

Love, Samba

With that, I folded the letter neatly, found an envelope and was just starting to wonder where I could buy a stamp near Marble Arch at this time on a Sunday when I stopped, re-opened the letter and read it again. I had been so naïve. There was no way I could send that letter to my sister in South Africa.

Any mail posted in England and addressed to my family in Durban would almost certainly be intercepted and read by the South African Police, and it would have been foolish to hand them, our enemy, details of my plans and information relating to SANROC.

This was the reality of my life in exile. I had grown accustomed to being wary of the authorities, but this was a different world. I would have to be careful of whatever I said and did, be suspicious of everyone I met, assume every telephone call was being bugged, not write anything on paper that could ever be used as evidence against me, my colleagues in London, or, above all, my friends and family at home.

So I sat down, and started to write again…

Portland Court Hotel
Marble Arch
London
March 21st, 1972

Dear Devi,

I hope everything is well. It has only been a week since I left South Africa, but I am already missing my life at home: my job, my friends, my sport, you and the family.

Everything is going well. I have got a teaching job east of London, and I am looking to get involved in coaching soon. I think I will settle down quickly.

Look after yourself, give my love to all and please write soon.

Love, Samba

That would have to do, for my family, and, probably, some bored Special Branch officer on mail duty. So I put this version in the envelope, and once again set off in search of a stamp near Marble Arch on a Sunday.

London seemed less daunting the second time around. Sidney Ling had once again proved a wonderful friend, offering me a teaching job at his school and a decent salary, and I was soon renewing old friendships and settling into a familiar routine. In general, people appeared to be aware of the situation in South Africa and, without saying much, seemed to understand the background to my return to England.

After a week or so as a non-paying guest at Chris de Broglio's hotel, I arranged to share a flat with Peter Slater, a friend I had met on a football coaching course at Loughborough in 1968. Four years on, we met for a drink, and, when he mentioned I could share a flat with him and some friends, I gratefully accepted the offer.

Peter was an Oxford University graduate playing football for British Universities when we first met, but he had since begun to work for the Football Association in Lancaster Gate, where he stayed for many years. We got on well and, as time passed, tended to move in many of the same circles.

SANROC was ticking along. Dennis Brutus had obviously left a huge gap when he accepted a teaching assignment in the US but Chris de Broglio and Jasmat Dhiraj, the former tennis player, had sustained various campaigns, exposing apartheid in sport. Nonetheless, Chris seemed pleased to accept my offer of voluntary assistance whenever I could spare the time.

We focused on two main goals: first, to isolate South African sport and, second, to consolidate that isolation by ensuring South Africa was actually expelled from the various international bodies.

By the early 1970s, we had made substantial progress towards the first target because, with the notable exception of rugby union, South Africa was no longer competing at international level in any major team sport. South Africa's recognition by the IOC had already been withdrawn in 1970.

However, we had made little headway in the second challenge because, in 1972, South Africa remained a full, albeit inactive, member of several international sports federations, including FIFA, the world governing body of football, FINA, the international swimming federation, and also of the IAAF, the ruling body of international athletics.

"It's a totally unacceptable situation," Chris de Broglio said, one Saturday morning as we sat together in the small SANROC office, still buried in the basement of his West End hotel.

I asked: "So, what's the plan?"

"We must go to the Olympic Games in Munich," he replied.

I immediately stopped what I was doing.

"Most of the major international federations hold congresses just prior to the Games," Chris continued. "The white South African sports officials will be there, talking about progress and putting their case. So, we must obviously be there as well. The FIFA congress is in Paris. The IAAF and FINA meetings are in Munich."

"Can we afford to go?"

"It should be OK," he said. "SANROC will pay for your airfare, and a bit of subsistence, but you'll need to take some of your own money as well and generally live as cheaply as possible."

"No problem," I replied.

The 1972 Olympic Games fell neatly into the English schools' summer holidays, so there was no need for me to request special leave from my responsibilities at school. This trip would be my first exposure to sport at the highest level. I was excited, and also quite apprehensive because I knew very few people.

I need not have worried.

I travelled to Paris and, arriving at the hotel hosting the FIFA congress, met Mourad Fahmy, Secretary-General of the Confederation of African

Football (CAF), an Egyptian who would later be succeeded in the same position by his son, Mustapha.

"Pleased to meet you," I said, shaking his hand.

"You're very welcome," Mourad replied, smiling. "Please make yourself at home here. We have a small office, feel free to use our facilities. You're one of us. Anything we can do, let us know."

So, I set off into the maze of football officials from around the world, drifting through the circuit of full congress sessions and bilateral meetings, snatched conversations in foyers, introductions at receptions. This was the oiled machinery of sports administration, which I would grow to know so well in years to come.

The following day, I met the newly elected President of CAF, Ydnekatcheou Tessema, from Ethiopia, and took the opportunity to explain to him why we felt it was important that South Africa should be expelled from FIFA. He wholly agreed.

"The issue is Stanley Rous," Tessema continued, explaining how the then FIFA President would not permit any expulsion motion because, like many western leaders at the time, he simply regarded any move against South Africa as a communist plot.

"We must bide our time," he concluded, before taking us off to another function where we would meet more people.

I explained the South African situation to anyone who would listen. Some people were clearly not interested, which surprised me. Maybe naïvely, I assumed everyone at FIFA would be keen to oppose apartheid. I was wrong. The world of sport was a more complicated place than I had imagined.

Arriving in Munich six days before the Olympics were due to start, I had found the Olympic community divided by the issue of Rhodesia. Many western countries believed the white-ruled country, excluded from Mexico City in 1968 after its Unilateral Declaration of Independence from Britain, should be allowed back into the fold to compete in Munich; all the African countries vigorously disagreed.

Avery Brundage, the 84-year-old American presiding over his last Olympics as President of the IOC, was determined the western view would prevail and, much to our surprise, we discovered the Rhodesian team was settled in the Athletes' Village.

Dennis Brutus had arrived in Munich a few days earlier, and the two of us participated in the African deliberations, arguing that Rhodesia's re-admission would encourage the apartheid regime, and that the whites-only team should be sent home.

The SANROC voice was heard and, importantly, was supported by both Abraham Ordia, a key member of the Olympic movement in Nigeria and then President of the Supreme Council of Sport in Africa (SCSA), and Jean-Claude Ganga, its Secretary-General. Hour by hour, with each telephone call and clandestine meeting, the first seeds of African solidarity at the Olympics were being sown.

"Would you be prepared to withdraw?" Ordia asked.

"Yes," came the replies, one by one.

Eventually, Ordia stepped forward and told Brundage that, if the Rhodesians were allowed to stay, all the African countries would withdraw from the Games. Ordia and Ganga then played their trump card, calling on the support of countries in the Eastern bloc. When they, too, threatened to join the boycott, Brundage was beaten.

On the eve of the opening ceremony, the Rhodesian team was asked to leave Munich.

The 1972 Olympics were ultimately defined by the terrorist assault on the Israeli team, which left 15 people dead and prompted the notoriously blunt Brundage to reflect how the Games had suffered from "two savage attacks".

We could not believe our ears. The IOC president had publicly equated Africa's efforts to expel Rhodesia with the murder of the Israelis. The US marathon gold medallist, Frank Shorter, was embarrassed, branding Brundage 'a pompous ass', and the Africans demanded an immediate apology for his remark.

This was quickly forthcoming, and Brundage slipped morosely into retirement, to be replaced as IOC President by Lord Killanin. In Munich, in 1972, the African members of the IOC had flexed their collective muscles for the first time, not the last.

I moved on to attend the meeting of the IAAF in Munich, where we were disappointed to find more compliant attitudes to South Africa among delegations from western countries, like Britain and the US.

It appeared as though, in their eyes, the world was divided into communists, who were their enemies, and everyone else, who were, by definition, their friends. So, the West was prepared to overlook apartheid, appease South Africa as a 'friend', and focus all their efforts on confronting the communist threat.

Our arguments seemed to dissolve in the broader political debate and, although South Africans were effectively excluded from the international athletics circuit because other Africans refused to compete alongside them, we soon realised the IAAF was not ready to expel South Africa.

Quite apart from other factors, the ruling body of international athletics retained a loaded voting system where the familiar powers like Britain, the USA and Germany had ten votes each, and most African nations each had to be content with just one.

The meeting of FINA, the world governing body of swimming, in Munich, was more encouraging.

Once again, it would obviously have been pointless to argue for South Africa's expulsion but, perhaps feeling more confident in a sport I knew well, I managed to put forward a proposal that, prior to any debate on expulsion, FINA should dispatch a fact-finding group to assess the status of swimming in South Africa.

The African officials liked the concept, drove the process and, in what was probably my first concrete achievement at this level of international sport, we secured the backing of FINA President Javier Ostos, of Mexico. The visit to South Africa was duly arranged. At last, I felt as though my presence in Munich was worthwhile.

I was not content to be a tourist, shaking hands and enjoying my surroundings. I needed to be achieving something for the cause that I had chosen to pursue. That cause, I told people over and over again, was the isolation of apartheid sport and, consequently, the creation of equal opportunities for all South Africans.

"Hello, I'm Sam Ramsamy, from SANROC."

"Er, hello."

"Yes, we're campaigning against apartheid in sport."

I soon developed a tough skin. When people were oblivious to the reality at home, I persisted. When people tried to change the subject, I kept talking. When people branded me as a communist puppet, I stayed focused on apartheid in sport.

If we found disinterest and sometimes outright opposition, we also found true friends. In Munich, I met Henry Adefope, leader of the Nigerian delegation at the Games and later a member of the IOC, and Jean-Claude Ganga, of the Congo, and Mustapha Larfaoui, of Algeria, later President of FINA: all three of these men would play important roles.

Of course, beyond the greetings and meetings, there were also the Olympic Games, the greatest sporting show on earth.

My earliest Olympic memory stretched back to Helsinki in 1952, when I followed the progress of two South Africans: Willie Toweel, who fought his way through to win a bronze medal in the flyweight boxing division and Joan Harrison, who won a gold medal in the 100m backstroke and, who, happily, even today, I deeply admire.

I eagerly read the newspaper reports from the Games of Melbourne in 1956, Rome in 1960, Tokyo in 1964 and Mexico City in 1968, never daring to dream that one day I would actually attend the Olympics in person.

Yet, here I was in Munich, and, even without any official kind of accreditation, the various African delegations helped me secure tickets to all the events I wanted to see. My natural inclination was to enjoy the exploits of the great African runners.

I had read all about Kipchoge Keino, the uncoached goat herder from the Nandi tribe in Kenya, who had got stuck in a traffic jam on his way to the 1 500m final at the 1968 Olympics, got out of the car and jogged the last mile to the stadium, and then found the energy to beat US favourite Jim Ryan and win the gold medal.

Four years on, I saw Keino advance through the heats and made sure I was in the Olympic stadium to watch his defence of the title in the 1 500m final. The Kenyan made his move after 600 metres, but he was tracked by Pekka Vasala. The dogged Finn took the lead in the home stretch, and won gold by three metres. Nowadays, Kip Keino is my colleague, a fellow member of the IOC.

Two days later, I sat in the same stadium and watched John Akii-Bua, of Uganda, take the lead in the 400m hurdles final and win the gold medal in a world record time of 47,82 seconds. I recall he was so thrilled that, after crossing the finish line, John just kept on running and cleared another two sets of hurdles.

On September 3rd, I had been visiting some members of the Nigerian delegation and was leaving the Athletes' Village when I saw a bustling huddle of media and TV cameras. I asked somebody what was happening, and was told that two top American athletes were holding a press conference after being disqualified.

Rey Robinson and Eddie Hart were both serious contenders in the 100m sprint, but they arrived late for the quarterfinals because they were working off an out-of-date, 18-month-old event schedule. Angry and indignant, they were letting off steam.

When a blond-haired, blue-eyed Ukrainian sprinter won the 100m gold medal the next day, the Americans claimed the absence of their top runners downgraded the victory. Valeriy Borzov ignored the sour grapes, and turned his attention to the 200m.

Running in the first semifinal, Borzov turned and spoke to the American, Larry Burton, as he passed him with 50 metres left; and he then completed an historic sprint double, rocketing past Larry Black, another American, to win the 200m final.

He refused to attend the post-race press interview, justifiably stating he had been badly treated by US journalists after his victory in the 100m. They portrayed him as a communist robot, but Borzov was anything but. "I very often feel as though I simply have to run," he once explained. "I might be walking along the street, dressed in a suit, but I feel that urge. Then convention gets the upper hand, and I manage to restrain myself."

Borzov later married Lyudmila Turischeva, a Russian gymnast who won even more Olympic medals than he did. He was elected as a member of the IOC a year before I was, in 1994, and we have since become close friends.

Thus, the Munich Olympics proved a defining experience for me, as my first experience of a major international sports event and also as the catalyst for many valued friendships.

Soon after returning to London, and settling back in what then seemed the humdrum rhythm of the Richard Alibon School in Dagenham, I received some sad, though not totally unexpected, news from home: Adrian Liversage had died of cancer.

I reacted with sadness, because he was a good man who had given me important advice, but also with a measure of relief because his passing meant I was free to explain to my family and friends exactly why I had decided to leave South Africa so suddenly.

When my friends wrote and asked whether I thought I would ever return home, I had to be honest and tell them it would probably not be possible until the end of apartheid.

At that moment, I mentally drew a line between my old life in South Africa and my new life in London. It was painful, because my family and friends remained on the other side of that line, but it was a necessary sacrifice. I had to accept it and move on.

I believed that, one day, I would return to South Africa, and I constantly bore in mind the advice that many other people in a similar position had given me, specifically that one must not develop roots in exile or it would be difficult to go home when the time came.

Towards the end of 1972, spending another Saturday morning at the SANROC office, Chris de Broglio surprised me again.

"Sam, last year, contacts of ours in East Germany offered to host a nominee from SANROC on a nine-month coaching course in Leipzig," he said. "I didn't know anyone who would be suitable then, but maybe you could go?"

"Perhaps," I replied.

"I think it could be a great opportunity," he insisted.

It did sound interesting. I had met Georg Zorowka, President of the East German Swimming Federation, in Munich and, in fact, had marshalled African votes to get him elected to the FINA Bureau in return for supporting our stand on South Africa.

Beyond that, my knowledge of East Germany was minimal but I was eager to grasp every opportunity to broaden my knowledge and, the following Monday morning, I was knocking on Sidney Ling's office door, enquiring about a year of absence. He agreed and, early in 1973, I arranged to book my flight to Berlin.

Another adventure beckoned, and I spent time in the library, researching my next destination. I learned how Germany was split after the Second World War and how, in May 1949, a congress of the Socialist Unity party

(SED) formally adopted the constitution of the German Democratic Republic (GDR).

Centralised government continued during the 1950s, but food shortages sparked an uprising in 1953 that was only suppressed by the intervention of Soviet forces. In 1961, the ruling SED Council of State authorised the building of a wall in the divided city of Berlin, to reduce the flow of people from east to west and consolidate East Germany as an independent country in its own right.

Economic growth followed, bringing self-confidence, ambitious build-ing programmes, eminence within the communist bloc, trade and, in 1973, membership of the United Nations.

In addition, the government took a decision that international sport would be the arena where this small country of 17 million people could define its identity, earn global respect and compete with the strongest nations. Resources were poured into coaching, new facilities and talent-identification programmes.

Erich Honecker had been elected as the first Secretary of the SED in 1971, and had been relaxing state control on intellectual and cultural activ-ities when an anxious South African teacher arrived in the Arrivals area at Berlin Airport and looked around.

"Mr Ramsamy?" said a middle-aged man, in halting English.

I nodded, and smiled.

"OK," he said, evidently relieved. "I'm from the College. We must hurry or you will miss your train to Leipzig."

As we scurried to the rail station, he told me I was welcome in the GDR and said I would be met at the station in Leipzig. My first impression of a communist country was positive: the sun was shining, people seemed busy and happy, belying the old stereotype of miserable poverty in a grim, austere landscape.

However, having arrived in Leipzig, and finding a trolley for my suitcase, I wondered if there was anyone there to meet me. I walked up and down the platform for about 10 minutes, becoming increasingly anxious about what I should do next in this strange place.

Eventually, I became aware of an athletic, young, dark-haired woman on the same platform. She was looking at me, and I glanced across at her.

We both hesitated, and then smiled.

"Is it Mr Ramsamy?"

"Yes."

"Hello," she said, striding across towards me, stretching out her arm to shake my hand. "I am Helga Zimmermann. Welcome."

I suppose everybody meets his or her spouse in a different way, but that bright Saturday morning at Leipzig station, I was certainly not expecting to meet the lady with whom I was destined to spend the rest of my life. Yet, that is what happened.

"Did you have a good trip?" she asked.

"It was fine, thank you."

We chatted easily as we drove to the campus, and it emerged that Helga had been a leading women's basketball player at international level, and was now attached to the college. She took me to the Hall of Residence, and introduced me to a Ugandan called Robert who showed me around.

Realising I was carrying very little money, she was also kind enough to advance me a few marks so I would be able to go out and buy myself some food over the weekend.

On Monday morning, I fulfilled the formalities of registration and quickly became absorbed in what proved to be an intensive and stimulating course, covering techniques of swimming coaching and the wider sports science strategy in East Germany.

As the weeks turned to months, I settled down and started to enjoy both the people and the lifestyle in Leipzig.

I don't deny it.

Furthermore, I saw advantages in the social system.

I don't deny that either.

In fact, I would say that, in 1973, in entirely political terms, I could have described myself as a communist.

The mere mention of that word has always provoked a wide range of responses in different people; for many white South Africans in the 1970s and 1980s, there was no greater evil. I use the word without emotion, simply to describe a political philosophy.

I am certainly not oblivious to the excesses of the communist system in East Germany. Measures such as the unlimited authority of the state security police, the Stasi, the compilation of an index containing the political history of every adult and the adoption of an authoritarian labour system were indefensible.

By the same token, I cannot ignore the more positive aspects of what I saw with my own eyes during 1973.

There was no unemployment, nobody was homeless, nobody was starving: such issues affected ordinary people.

In many developing countries, popular politics is defined, not by grand plans for democracy, but by daily issues of security: will I get a job, will I have somewhere to live, will I be looked after when I am old, can I walk safely down the street, etc.

There are different types of freedom. They may not have been 'free' in the western sense of the word, but the East German people were free from the fear of poverty, and they became part of a small nation that developed the 10th largest economy in the world and produced many fine scientists, musicians and athletes.

This is not a defence of Communism – I have spent most of my life campaigning for democracy – but it would be wrong to suggest the East German system was an unequivocal failure.

Sport was a central element of the national plan and, through the 1970s, as many as 10 000 East German athletes were involved in a state-sponsored attempt to create a sports power to rival the United States of America and the Soviet Union.

The results are a matter of record: at Munich in 1972, the German Democratic Republic finished third in the final medal table, with 20 gold, 23 silver and 23 bronze; at Montreal in 1976, the GDR took second place, ahead of the USA, with 40 gold, 25 silver and 25 bronze. They retained second place at Moscow in 1980, then joined the boycott of Los Angeles in 1984, and reclaimed second place at Seoul in 1988, with 37 gold, 35 silver and 30 bronze. These are extraordinary results.

Some of these medals were probably secured by the use of drugs. It has been documented that up to 1 200 former East German athletes have experienced health problems associated with the use of banned steroids, including heart disease, testicular and breast cancer, depression and eating disorders. Some female athletes have reported miscarriages.

A series of former GDR coaches were prosecuted in 2000 and the unified German government established a compensation fund of U$2,5 million for the doping victims of East German sport.

The institutional distribution of drugs is beyond doubt, but the East Germans were far from the only sinners. There are some who believe Eastern bloc drugs scandals have been exaggerated to divert attention from the drugs culture in the West. In my view, the only difference lay in the channels of distribution: the cheating pills were handed out by officials in the GDR, and sold by shady, private dealers in the USA and elsewhere.

Having noted all this, the drugs issue ought not obscure the fact that East German talent-identification structures have become standard practice in many countries today.

These systems have been characterised as ruthless conveyor belts for brainwashed, bewildered teenagers, selected by a process of mass screening. This image is completely false.

In fact, gifted youngsters were encouraged, not forced, to attend special sports schools, and later given funding and specialist training to realise their full sporting potential.

East Germany, like other countries, did cheat by using banned drugs but, even without such activity, the excellence of their system would have earned an exceptional haul of medals.

Operation Excellence, the talent identification system that I devised for NOCSA, which has produced champions like Penny Heyns, Hezekiel Sepeng and others, is based on an East German model blended with elements of the American universities structure.

In simple terms, instead of distributing funds directly to the federations, money and time is spent on enhancing the coaching and training environment of specific elite athletes.

For example, arrangements may be made for a young sprinter to finish his university degree in six years, rather than four, giving him more time for his training programme. Or a talented group of swimmers might be sent on an intensive four-month course with a world-class coach at a specially equipped facility.

Such specialist activity was happening in East Germany in the 1970s, and it is starting to happen in South Africa today.

Towards the end of my stay in Leipzig, I called Chris de Broglio in London and asked whether I could represent SANROC at a FINA meeting in Belgrade. The governing body of international swimming was preparing to debate the report of the fact-finding trip to South Africa, which I had prompted in Munich.

I was granted leave from my studies and, having collected my ticket at Leipzig, flew to the capital of Yugoslavia.

The effort proved worthwhile, because the fact-finding team presented a damning report of apartheid's effect on South African swimming. I worked hard and, with the support of Georg Zorowka and Mustapha Larfaoui, who helped me talk to the right people and create the right climate, projected a strong case.

The Bureau duly voted to expel South Africa and, even if the formal decision could only be taken by the full FINA Congress at its meeting in 1976, prior to the Olympics in Montreal, I was thrilled by developments and the message it sent to Pretoria.

My goal was to fight apartheid in sport and, at last, I had matched my words with some cast-iron deeds. I returned to Leipzig, feeling more positive than ever before, and made the most important decision of my life.

To be honest, I liked the look of Helga Zimmermann as soon as I spotted her looking for me at Leipzig station. More than 30 years later, to be honest, I still like the look of her.

Through force of circumstances, losing my mother when I was very young and then living overseas, I had spent most of the first 33 years of my life alone. In many ways, I had grown used to being alone. Helga ensured I would never be alone again.

We quickly became friends at College and, within only a few months, our relationship had become intense. During the week spent in Belgrade, I realised I was in love with her and, as soon as I returned to Leipzig, I asked Helga to marry me.

She said yes.

"Think about this very seriously," said Chris de Broglio, when I told him the news. "You are not only marrying into a different race, but also into a different culture. It won't be easy."

My friend had my best interests at heart – and, it's true, there cannot have been too many relationships between South Africans of Indian origin and East German basketball stars – but I told him we were compatible, and that was most important. We realised many obstacles lay ahead, but we would overcome them.

I was initially concerned how Helga's family would react to the news. The Zimmermanns were close-knit and conservative and, while there were not many black people in the city of Leipzig, there were even fewer black prospective sons-in-law.

My anxieties were misplaced, and I was welcomed with open arms by her parents, Lisbeth and Erich, and her sister, Ursula. Ever since, they have been nothing less than family to me.

In fact, we never encountered any racial prejudice at all in and around Leipzig. There were no derogatory remarks aimed at us and we were never thrown out of any restaurants. On the contrary, we were embraced by ordinary East German people.

Strangely, in years to come, we would find greater resistance to our 'mixed marriage' in certain parts of England.

Our initial plan was to get married within a couple of months and, when my course ended, settle in London. However, it quickly became clear this timetable was wildly optimistic.

First, in East Germany at the time, only the State had the authority to issue marriage licences, so we needed to get official permission. We filled out the forms, and waited.

Second, the country's emigration policy was restrictive. Higher living standards in the West prompted a flood across the border in the late 1950s, and, with few exceptions, emigration had been very difficult ever since. Infamously, many desperate men and women would try to scale the Berlin Wall and be shot dead.

Helga and I decided to apply through the correct channels, and so we waited, and we waited, and we waited. In the end, when my course ended, I had to return to London without Helga.

We waited... at one stage, we approached the leaders of the African National Congress in exile, and asked them to intervene on our behalf with the East German authorities.

Still we waited, talking on the telephone each Sunday... then, Abraham

Ordia, the President of the Supreme Council for Sport in Africa, agreed to assist and added his voice to our case.

Still we waited, with equal patience and resolve.

The weeks became months, and the months became years. I used to travel to Leipzig twice a year, during the summer and then at Christmas; and still we waited, and waited.

It became apparent that our application was being blocked by the Director of the Institute where Helga was teaching. He believed she was going to the 'capitalist West' with the intention of giving away her specialist knowledge of East German sport.

We persisted, and still we waited. Maybe the officials wanted to see if our relationship would stand the test of time. It did and, in the end, the papers arrived: we were allowed to marry in Leipzig, and Helga was permitted to emigrate to London.

A process that we had initially hoped would take four months had ultimately taken almost four years.

Finally, on June 11th, 1977, we were married in Leipzig, with Helga's family in attendance. I had to be content with sending the wedding photographs home to my family in Durban.

We have been together ever since.

Through three decades, Helga has been more than a source of support to me. She has been a genuine partner, always sharing my commitment to SANROC and then to NOCSA.

When we compiled the so-called blacklist of athletes who had competed in or against South Africans, it was Helga who endlessly scoured the results columns of the British and South African newspapers to ensure the blacklist was constantly accurate and up to date.

Whenever we faced any particular problem or dilemma, Helga would always get involved, take time to understand the situation or the issue and, invariably in private, offer her advice.

Even now, whenever I write a letter or prepare a speech, I am not happy until Helga has checked and approved it.

I don't know where I would be without her.

We realised from an early stage that we might not be able to have children, because Helga had suffered peritonitis following several operations early in her basketball career, but we have always been extremely close to our nephews and nieces.

Otherwise, it has been, is and will be just Helga and I.

ALLIES

Without friends, we would have meandered around the conferences and congresses of world sport, getting nowhere. With friends, friends who helped us plan, friends who provided access, friends in high places, friends who often put their careers on the line for our cause, SANROC made progress.

The campaign was yielding dividends.

We promoted motions calling for South Africa's expulsion from international governing bodies, and we organised boycotts if South Africans were permitted to compete. This visible barrage increased awareness of apartheid and applied genuine pressure on the National Party government in Pretoria.

Through more than two decades, the anti-apartheid sports movement played an essential role in the broader struggle. As such, those people who supported and sustained the campaign must be recognised for their role in South Africa's liberation.

Recognition is important, and often contested. Many accounts of this period have been written, each projecting a different version of what happened and who should take the credit.

This is the nature of history. If four people gather in one place and talk for an hour, and each of them is then asked to outline what was said, the result will be four different accounts.

All anyone can do is offer his or her own perspective, honestly and sincerely, and that is what I set out to do here.

My own assessment reflects events that took place after 1972, when I became actively involved, and it recognises that very many people made vital contributions. I hope to mention as many as possible in these reflections.

However, I will identify four individuals, who were central to everything we achieved and who have not been awarded the recognition they deserve. It is important for South Africans to recognise these people who worked so hard to create conditions that many of them take for granted today.

In no particular order, these revered allies are Abraham Ordia, our fixer from Nigeria, Ydnekatcheou Tessema, our tactician from Ethiopia, Jean-Claude Ganga, our orator from the Congo, and Abdel Mohamed Halim, our patron from Sudan.

Abraham Ordia – The Fixer

In a tight situation, in a closely contested vote, Abraham Ordia was someone you always wanted to have on your side.

He was a very powerful man from a very powerful country, and I knew him so well that I used to call him 'Dad'.

Abraham is credited with laying the foundations of organised sport in Nigeria, when he helped to establish the National Sports Commission in 1963 and became its first Secretary.

I first met him at the 1972 Olympic Games in Munich, when he was General-Secretary of the Nigerian Olympic Committee and President of the Supreme Council for Sport in Africa (SCSA), two posts he held for many years.

"Apartheid is a crime against all Africans," he told me. "It isn't only a matter for South Africans. It represents a challenge to us all, and every African must be ready to join the struggle."

It didn't take me long to recognise that when Abraham went ahead, the political might of Nigeria followed; and wherever Nigeria went, many other African countries invariably followed.

In 1976, in his capacity as President of the SCSA, he visited New Zealand with the intention of engaging the government that tacitly supported sporting ties with white South Africa. In the event, he was insulted by the Prime Minister, Robert Muldoon.

Abraham was not a man to aggravate. Three weeks later, he ensured that Nigeria led the African boycott of the 1976 Olympic Games, in protest against the New Zealand rugby tour of South Africa.

At every stage of the campaign, at Gleneagles, at the Olympics, at Commonwealth meetings, this strong, committed man was to be found at the centre of the action, fighting for South Africa.

There were many occasions when events seemed to be going against us, and Abraham would make some telephone calls, fix the problem and somehow hold everything together.

If a situation required firm words, Abraham had the strength of character and confidence to step forward.

In October 1982, the Commonwealth Games Federation met at Marlborough House, London, before the 12th Games, scheduled for Brisbane, Australia, and issued a statement that said any country whose sporting teams or individuals competed either in or against South Africa would be liable for sanction.

Two nations abstained from supporting the motion: England, because they said the statement was 'too restrictive', and Nigeria, which told the media that the final wording was 'a joke'.

Ordia recognised the need to seize the agenda, and raged to the Press: "Nigeria has always been a frontrunner in campaigning for the sporting isolation of South Africa, but this statement is watered down. It is colonial in tone. It has no teeth and the Commonwealth has no machinery to police it."

He was loyal to the cause, and he was loyal to me personally, always taking care to assist me wherever possible, especially when my peculiar status, as a representative of SANROC rather than any country, placed me in an awkward position.

In November 1982, on the 20th anniversary of its decision to pass resolution 1761 recommending sanctions against South Africa, the United Nations General Assembly presented awards to seven persons in recognition of their outstanding contribution to the global movement for sanctions against apartheid.

They were Houari Boumediene of Algeria, Romesh Chandra of India, Jeanne Martin-Cissé of Guinea, Father Trevor Huddleston of Britain, Dr Martin Luther King of the USA, Jan Nico Scholten of the Netherlands and… Chief Abraham Ordia, of Nigeria.

If ever anyone deserved to see the results of their labours, it was him. Sadly, Abraham Ordia died in 1995, a year after South Africa buried apartheid and celebrated liberation.

Jean-Claude Ganga – The Orator

If we had a case to make and an audience in their seats, the man we always wanted to approach the podium and make a speech with real passion and presence was Jean-Claude Ganga.

Blessed with strong features and a booming voice, this sports leader from the Congo stepped forward to speak for the liberation of South African sport many times, and always excelled.

I met Jean-Claude at the same meeting where I met Abraham Ordia, at Munich in 1972. He spoke no English and I spoke no French, so we needed the services of a translator.

It is often said that everything suffers in translation except a bishop, but we nurtured a strong empathy and understanding from that initial meeting, and have remained close ever since.

We worked together in Montreal, arranging the African boycott of the 1976 Olympic Games, operating from Jean-Claude's room at the Elizabeth Hotel. I often used to sit up during the night, waiting for telephone calls, while he and his wife had a few hours sleep a few metres away.

At meeting after meeting, the anti-apartheid sports movement found its most persuasive, boldest voice in Ganga.

His extraordinary speech to the Congress of the International Amateur Athletic Federation in 1976 was generally regarded as the decisive factor in winning the vote to expel South Africa.

Two years later, just before the FIFA World Cup in Argentina, he spoke in support of a proposal to expel Taiwan and admit China to FIFA. The motion failed, but he energised the Congress.

Afterwards, Jean-Claude and I were standing outside the hall when we were approached by two Englishmen. "That was a superb speech," said one.

Jean-Claude thanked them and asked: "Where are you from?"

"England," they replied.

"That's nice," he said, and seemed to lose interest.

When the two men had dissolved back into the milling crowd, I asked Jean-Claude if he knew the two Englishmen. He said he had never met them before, still seeming quite unconcerned.

"Well," I said. "That was Alan Wade, the English coach, and Sir Stanley Rous, the former President of FIFA."

He looked aghast, asking: "Why didn't you tell me?"

We laughed then, and we were still laughing in 1991, when he played an important leadership role in the complex negotiations that led to the unification of South African sport.

SANROC campaigns took me around the globe: clockwise from left, visiting John Minto, middle, and David Wickham, left, of the Stop The Tour Campaign in New Zealand, 1979; addressing the United Nations Commission on Apartheid in New York; launching my book on apartheid sport in Amsterdam with Dutch footballer Ruud Gullit in attendance.

Denis Howell proved to be one of the most effective and supportive British Ministers of Sport. Here, with two other fervent campaigners against apartheid, Sir Sridath Ramphal, Secretary-General of the Commonwealth, on his right, and Major General Joe Garba, Nigerian Foreign Minister, Denis is addressing a meeting at the Houses of Parliament in London.

Of all sports, rugby union was the most unwilling to isolate South Africa, but a few rugby men were prepared to support the protest. The former French international captain, Francois Moncla, joined me at an anti-apartheid conference in Paris.

Commonwealth meetings often proved a battleground between those wanting to isolate South African sport and those inclined to assist the Republic. At one such gathering, I was privileged to meet Queen Elizabeth II. Above, Her Majesty is greeting Mendi Msimang, who later became South Africa's High Commissioner in London, with Father Trevor Huddleston looking on.

My grandparents emigrated from India to South Africa, and I enjoyed my first visit to the subcontinent in 1987, when I also had the opportunity to meet the Indian Prime Minister, Rajiv Gandhi.

Clive Lloyd, the West Indian cricketer, standing left, famously said all the gold in South Africa would not persuade him to play in the land of apartheid. We are joined by Ismail Bhamjee, of Botswana.

Jasmat Dhiraj was recognised as South Africa's finest non-white tennis player, but he was denied the opportunity to represent his country in the Davis Cup. He eventually settled in London, where he became a member of the SANROC Executive.

SANROC's funding relied on the generosity of IDAF, the International Defence and Aid Fund, and on the kindness of many individuals and organisations around the world. Among these supporters are, clockwise from top left, Professor Bruce Kidd and Phyllis Berck in Canada, Helen McCue in Australia, Bobby Naidoo, one of my oldest friends and for many years Secretary-General of AIPS, the International Association of the Sports Press, and René Moustard, President of the FSGT, a sports organisation within the French labour movement.

We constantly relied on the help of friends such as, left, Dr Abdel Mohammed Halim, of the Sudan, a prominent member of the IOC, and, right, Gough Whitlam, the former Prime Minister of Australia.

Australia always provided a loyal, reliable ally for the movement against apartheid in sport. John Coates, left, now an IOC member, has always been supportive, and we were assisted at various stages by Kevan Gosper, an IOC member, above right, seated left, and the former Australian Minister of Foreign Affairs, Gareth Evans, above right, seated right.

After serving a term as the Congolese Ambassador to China, Jean-Claude returned to sport and was elected as a Member of the International Olympic Committee, and also as President of the Association of National Olympic Committees of Africa (ANOCA). In this role, he stepped forward to facilitate the unity talks.

Clever, sensitive and perceptive throughout, at one stage, he almost lost his patience with one group who were stalling on a final agreement. "Look," he exclaimed, "this train is getting ready to leave the station. If you don't jump aboard, it's going to leave without you and you will be left behind."

Thabo Mbeki, who met Jean-Claude on several occasions, was impressed when he heard about the comment and, from that day, he always called Jean-Claude 'the stationmaster'.

On another occasion, during a break in tense discussions, a South African playfully referred to the Congolese facilitator as a lion. "Just remember," Jean-Claude said, beaming. "When a lion shows you his teeth, it does not mean he's smiling."

In 1999, sadly, Jean-Claude was investigated and expelled as a member of the IOC. However, this cheerful, larger-than-life figure deserves to be remembered not for the allegations that he solicited bribes from candidate cities bidding to host the Olympics, but for his heroic contribution to the abolition of apartheid in sport.

Ydnekatcheou Tessema – The Tactician

A crucial part of winning any conflict is choosing when and where to fight. During the 1970s and 1980s, our primary tactician was a man universally hailed as the father of sport in Ethiopia.

At stages, the Minister of Sport, President of the African Football Confederation, a member of the IOC and a member of the Supreme Council for Sport in Africa, Ydnekatcheou used his excellent contacts to gauge the precise timing of our initiatives.

"Maybe we can table a motion to expel South Africa," I would ask in advance of, for example, a FIFA Congress.

"No," Ydnekatcheou would respond. "I don't believe we can get enough votes to win. We must be patient."

We would listen and wait because we understood that to put forward a motion, and lose, would serve only to encourage the supporters of apartheid. "SANROC and communists defeated," the apologists of white South Africa would have gloated.

Ydnekatcheou established his reputation in football, first as a respected international player, then as a successful coach of the champion St George club side and also of the Ethiopian team that won the third African Cup of Nations in 1963.

He also made an enormous, historic contribution to athletics in his country, establishing the structures that eventually produced the likes of Abebe Bikila, who won the Olympic marathon at Rome in 1960 and successfully defended his title in Tokyo four years later, and many other legendary Ethiopian runners.

Fluent in four languages, calm and shrewd by nature, he was always enthusiastic and always involved. Typically, while coaching the Ethiopian football team, he used to rush from the changing room to the press box to do the match commentary for radio. He launched the first Ethiopian sports office in 1943 and then, in 1957, became one of 15 founding members of the Confederation of African Football (CAF) at Khartoum, Sudan. In that historic meeting, he established his credentials as a scourge of apartheid.

Officials of the white South African football federation were also present as founding members of CAF, but, amid the bonhomie, Ydnekatcheou insisted any South African team competing in the first African Cup of Nations had to be open to all races.

When the South Africans refused and withdrew, Ydnekatcheou successfully argued for their immediate suspension.

"FIFA were not at all happy with that decision," he once told me, "and we received a formal complaint stating we had no right to suspend a FIFA member from our Confederation.

"In response, we launched a campaign to expel South Africa from FIFA and, at the congress in Tokyo in 1964, Ethiopia, Egypt and Ghana co-sponsored a motion to this effect.

"The timing of our move was perfect because, since Argentina and Mexico were competing to host the 1970 World Cup, both sides were eager to secure the votes of the African bloc and they both openly supported our proposal to expel South Africa.

"Sir Stanley Rous, the FIFA President, stepped in and ruled that South Africa would be suspended from playing international matches, but not expelled. As Africans, we realised South Africa would never be expelled until FIFA had a new president."

Ydnekatcheou and I became extremely close friends over the years, until his death on August 20th, 1987, but, even now, whenever I am in Addis Ababa, I take care to visit his family.

After all he did for us, it is the least I can do for him.

Dr Abdel Mohamed Halim – The Patron

If there was ever a major development within the IOC or one of the major federations, we were usually given the news by an educated, gentle and highly committed physician from the Sudan.

Dr Halim was one of the first Africans to be elected a member of the IOC, and, after helping the likes of Tessema to launch CAF, he served as President of the Confederation from 1968 to 1972, and stepped in as Acting President from 1987 to 1988 before the appointment of Issa Hayatou.

Of almost equal importance to those of us at SANROC, Dr Halim's son was working as a medical doctor in London, which meant this extremely influential and very sympathetic African sports leader was always a frequent visitor to the British capital, and our office.

If the white South African officials had made a presentation to the IOC, Dr Halim gave us the details. If South Africa's supporters were marshalling support at FIFA, Dr Halim suggested how we should counter the move.

Nothing compelled him to be so obliging and certainly nobody paid him. He repeatedly went out of his way to help us, over two decades, because he believed our cause was just.

At the IOC session of 1970, he delivered an important speech during the heated debate on whether the IOC should withdraw its recognition of South Africa as a member of the Olympic movement.

This excerpt from his address illustrates the line of his argument in an era when it was widely regarded as absolutely taboo to mix sport and politics, and shows his steady, persuasive nature.

"This question of South Africa is not taken at all in a political way, neither are we interfering with the political set-up in South Africa. As you and I know, there are some countries that practise racial discrimination in politics and in other ways of life. This is not our concern, because they did not bring this discrimination into sport. In so doing, they have observed the Olympic ideals, and nobody can hold an offence to them.

"The only question is whether South Africa conforms to the rules and regulations of the International Olympic Committee. Does it conduct its activity in accordance with the Olympic Charter?

"Look at the emblem there, which signifies not black and white, but all colours and which means unity and not the division between races. Baron de Coubertin acted for the poor as well as for the rich, for the haves and the have-nots, for the oppressed as well as for those who are oppressing. He acted to bring them altogether in the Olympic ideals..."

At this point, Dr Halim was interrupted by the patrician tones of Lord Luke of Pavenham, an IOC member from Britain.

"Could I ask a question? In most of the points he has made, it is the government at fault and not the athletes or the Olympic committee and the athletes. Are they to suffer? Are we urging them to break the law in their country, and if they won't break the law, then they have to be thrown out?"

Dr Halim said: "We're not asking them to disobey the laws of their country. We ask you to obey the laws of your Committee."

"The sufferers will be the very people we say we want to help," bellowed Lord Luke, indignantly.

"Sometimes you beat your child very severely in order to put him right," countered Dr Halim, as the President called order.

The vote was taken soon afterwards, and the IOC withdrew its recognition of South Africa by a wide margin. Dr Halim's reason had won the day.

Abraham Ordia, Jean-Claude Ganga, Ydnekatcheou Tessema and Dr Abdel Mohammed Halim moved in many of the same circles for much of their lives in sport, and they all knew each other well.

Each of them made many sacrifices for the cause of liberating South African sport, some so visible that they made themselves highly unpopular in some quarters, many others unreported.

For all their commitment and dedication, each of their names should be recalled with honour and respect in perpetuity.

BOYCOTT IN MONTREAL

On Sunday June 13th, 1976, at an impassioned meeting of around 400 students in the Orlando district of Soweto, a young man named Tsietsi Mashinini, 19, stood up and suggested that a mass demonstration should take place on the following Wednesday.

The teenagers were objecting to the Afrikaans language being used as the medium of instruction in Soweto schools, and they made a pact not to tell any of their parents about their plans in case they tried to block them.

"Our parents are willing to suffer under the white man's rule," one student had written to *The World* newspaper the previous week. "They have been living for years under these laws and they have become immune to them, but we strongly refuse to swallow an education that is designed to make us slaves in the country of our birth."

On June 16th, more than 15 000 students, mostly dressed in school uniform, gathered at various points in the vast township south west of Johannesburg and began to march, all converging on the Orlando West secondary school, where they intended to stand and sing 'Nkosi Sikeleli 'iAfrika', register their protest and then quietly return to their homes.

A police squad was dispatched to confront the marchers as they started. They told the crowd to disperse but, when this order was ignored, dogs were unleashed and tear gas was fired. Students responded by throwing stones and bottles at the police. Journalists then witnessed a policeman draw his revolver and shoot, without warning, into the crowd. More shots were heard.

Chaos ensued. A small 13-year-old boy called Hector Pietersen was shot in the chest, and cradled away by Mbuyisa Makhubu. This specific scene was captured by Samuel Nzima, and his photograph was flashed around the globe, destined to become the abiding image of what is now known as the Soweto Uprising.

The dawn of June 17th unveiled a Sowetan landscape of burnt-out cars, gutted beer halls and bodies in the streets. The official death toll was 23, but others put it as high as 200.

Rioting blazed through the township for three frenzied days, and then quickly spread to other areas in the Transvaal, and to Durban and Cape Town. A new generation was raising its voice.

Barely nine days after the uprising, the New Zealand rugby team arrived in South Africa and, on June 30th, they won the first match of their tour, overcoming a Border Invitation XV 24-0 at the Basil Kenyon stadium in East London.

The 1976 All Blacks had set their hearts on becoming the first New Zealand team to win a Test series in South Africa and not even the blood on the streets of Soweto deterred them. The played on in blissful oblivion.

It was the concurrence of these two events – the massacre and the rugby tour – that outraged millions around the world, but especially the governments and the sports leaders of Africa. How, they asked, could New Zealand, in all conscience, insist upon sending their rugby team to a country where schoolchildren were being shot? There seemed no possible defence.

I knew what the rugby union officials would have said: they would have talked about standing by old friends and refusing to mix politics with sport, and they would have continued to conduct themselves like a secret society where loyalty towards each other was far, far more important than how their insular actions might affect anybody else.

Against this background of turmoil and raised emotions, the finest athletes in the world were steadily starting to arrive in Montreal, preparing for the Olympic Games, which were due to be opened on Saturday, July 17th, 1976.

I travelled to Canada as the SANROC representative, and was surprised to arrive and find IOC officials preoccupied by a dispute over Taiwan, rather than the African issue.

Pierre Trudeau, the Canadian Prime Minister, had provoked a problem when he bluntly refused entry visas to the Taiwanese team because he was keen to nurture close relations with China. The IOC strongly objected, but the hosts insisted and Taiwan stayed at home.

Lord Killanin was presiding over his first Olympics as the IOC President and, if the former journalist and sports official from Ireland had hoped to enjoy himself, he was disappointed.

Initially perturbed by the threat of labour strikes, Killanin spent most of his time in what proved to be a vain attempt to solve the Taiwanese situation. In footballing terms, he took his eye off the African ball.

So, when the government of Tanzania strongly protested against the participation of New Zealand athletes in Montreal, the IOC and its careworn President seemed not to notice.

History was repeating itself. The IOC had underestimated the strength of pan-African opposition to apartheid and its collaborators at Munich in 1972, when a boycott over Rhodesia was narrowly averted, and now, they were doing so again.

I arranged to meet Abraham Ordia and Jean-Claude Ganga, respectively the President and Secretary-General of the Supreme Council for Sport in Africa, to discuss what was quickly becoming a very serious situation.

"People are extremely angry," Ordia told me. "I have been talking to government officials in many African countries and they won't compete if the New Zealand team is allowed to stay. There is real determination to do something."

Dennis Brutus had arrived from the United States to help the cause, and our instinct was to find an option that would enable the Africans to make their protest, and yet still preserve the status of the Olympic Games. "Maybe African athletes could withdraw from any event where they come into direct competition with a New Zealander," he suggested.

"If an African boxer is drawn against a New Zealander, he could refuse to fight, or if an African runner is drawn in the same heat as a New Zealander, he could refuse to run. In this way, we would effectively isolate New Zealand and avoid calling a mass boycott."

Ganga had listened carefully. "Perhaps we haven't reached that stage," he said. "First, we should talk to the New Zealanders."

The next day, Jean-Claude asked me to join him at a clandestine meeting with Lance Cross, an IOC member and President of the New Zealand National Olympic Committee, and the widely admired Lord Porritt, an honorary member of the IOC and former Surgeon-General to the British Royal family.

We greeted each other amicably and settled in a small room. I was content to sit quietly, as my Congolese friend started to speak.

He stressed the seriousness of the developing crisis, and proposed a face-saving compromise for all sides: "If the All Blacks cut short their tour of South Africa and fly home now, I can guarantee all the African countries will stay here in Montreal and compete in the Games."

Cross responded: "You must understand that we have no jurisdiction over the New Zealand Rugby Union. It is not an Olympic sport."

"I know," Jean-Claude replied, "but you can talk to your government and the New Zealand Rugby Union. I read yesterday that two of the All Black players got caught too close to some kind of demonstration and suffered the effects of tear gas. Use that as a starting point. Just say you are stopping the tour to guarantee the safety of your players and officials."

After a moment's contemplation, Lord Porritt said he thought this was an excellent idea. Cross did not seem as enthusiastic but, at least, he said he would discuss our proposal with his government and get back to us with a decision, either way, as soon as possible. We never heard another word.

Events were gathering pace. The Organisation of African Unity (OAU) happened to be meeting in Mauritius and, the next day, we received news that the OAU had passed a resolution calling for African countries to withdraw from the Olympic Games if the New Zealanders took part.

"That's it then," I said to Jean-Claude.

"What?"

"A boycott is inevitable."

He nodded soberly. We took no delight in this realisation, and instead applied ourselves to our work, which had now changed from seeking a solution to coordinating the boycott. With its desk and telephone, Jean-Claude's hotel room became a makeshift office, and we worked hard to develop and pursue a strategy and also to ensure the free flow of information and debate between the stakeholders: government officials in capital cities around the continent, sports administrators and those teams who had already arrived and settled in the Athletes' Village.

I barely slept for three days. African solidarity proved to be a complicated construction, and we took great care to put the right blocks in the right places.

In each region of the continent, we needed a broadly 'acceptable' country to show the lead in announcing their withdrawal, making it easy for their neighbours to follow.

For example, in East Africa, we arranged for Kenya to withdraw before Uganda, because Uganda was then ruled by Idi Amin, and other nations might have been put off the boycott if it looked as if they were following him.

Similarly, in West Africa, the Congo was eager to take its athletes home, but it was known as a socialist, revolutionary state at the time. So, Jean-Claude set aside his patriotic instincts and telephoned two senior officials in the moderate Cameroon government, the Minister of Sport and Minister of Foreign Affairs, and arranged for them to move first and showed the way.

So it continued, hour after hour. The telephone rang relentlessly and, with a five-hour time difference between Canada and most African countries, our days merged blearily into nights. Yet, the jigsaw came together.

In the end, no fewer than 17 African countries decided to withdraw their athletes from the 1976 Olympic Games, and they were joined in this dramatic action by the sympathetic governments of Guyana and Iraq. In so doing, they delivered probably the single most visible and dramatic demonstration against apartheid sport.

African solidarity held. Tanzania, the strongest of the strong, never even sent their athletes to Montreal. Cameroon agreed to take part in the Opening Ceremony, in deference to Canada, their alphabetical neighbours and allies at the United Nations, but then withdrew. Egypt and Morocco also marched around the Olympic Stadium, and even participated in the first day's events, but then travelled home.

Only Senegal and the Ivory Coast opted to compete at the Games, prompting widespread suspicion that their governments retained covert links with South Africa. Members of their National Olympic Committees shrugged and said they had been ordered to stay in Montreal.

The greatest sacrifices were made by the athletes, men and women who had trained for many years to perform on an Olympic stage, but who surrendered that opportunity in the name of what they realised to be a greater cause.

Filbert Bayi, of Tanzania, the world record holder in the men's 1 500m, agreed to stay at home, leaving John Walker, ironically of New Zealand, to claim the gold medal for himself.

Such selfless gestures were made in support of the oppressed people of South Africa, and such sacrifices should not be forgotten.

The African boycott had been secured and implemented, but our work in Montreal was not complete, and we turned our attentions to the task of securing the formal expulsion of three whites-only South African sporting bodies from their respective international federations.

Encouraged by the prospect of completing the processes started four years earlier in Munich, we sat with our allies and agreed strategies to exclude South Africa from football, swimming, and athletics, and thus to hammer more nails into the coffin of apartheid sport.

We approached the FIFA Congress in Montreal with confidence because, two years earlier, Joao Havelange had been elected to succeed Sir Stanley Rous as FIFA President, and the Brazilian was a powerful and committed opponent of apartheid.

He had campaigned for election and secured total support from the African bloc by making two firm promises: first, he would ensure Africa was allocated a second berth in what was then a 16-nation World Cup final tournament; secondly, he would complete the expulsion of South Africa.

Havelange had proved as good as his word on the first matter, but we took nothing for granted on the second, because the FIFA constitution stipulated that a 75 percent majority was required for the Congress to expel a member nation.

Even in 1976, in the wake of the Soweto Uprising, South Africa enjoyed the support of many western officials, who still seemed to define every issue in terms of their ideological struggle with communism and the Soviet Union.

Meetings of the various Confederations preceded the full FIFA Congress, and we wheeled and dealt at these events, gathering support by trading African votes on other issues in return for support in expelling South Africa.

Ydnekatcheou Tessema, then President of the Confederation of African Football, was the expert in this practice and, on the eve of the meetings, he called me aside and asked me to attend the meeting of the Asian Football Confederation (AFC).

"We need to make a deal, Sam," Tessema said. "The AFC want Taiwan expelled from FIFA, so arrange to meet Dato Hamzah, of Malaysia, the AFC President, and tell him Africa will vote en bloc to expel Taiwan if the AFC nations agree to vote en bloc to expel South Africa."

I followed the instructions. The deal was done, even if Dato Hamzah did seem unsure whether we would deliver all the African votes.

In the event, with the backing of Havelange, the Socialist bloc and the Asians, the FIFA Congress voted to expel South Africa with the dissent of no more than nine countries.

We switched our focus to the governing body of swimming, where we needed the FINA Congress to ratify their own Bureau's decision to get rid of South Africa, taken in Belgrade in 1973.

The outcome was never in doubt, even though the FINA President, Harold Henning, of the USA, was reluctant to support the resolution.

I was present in the hall when the chairman concluded a brief debate by asking for a show of hands from the assembled delegates.

Hands were raised to my left and to my right. I felt a surge of exhilaration and vindication: this was my main sport and, to an extent, this vote was the result of my efforts over four years.

"The result is clear," the chairman declared immediately. "South Africa is expelled."

We were winning. In conference halls around Montreal, the 'oranje, blanje, blou' (the South African flag) was being lowered and world sport was standing firm against apartheid. Two down, one to go.

Our last, and most difficult, challenge was to persuade the IAAF, then known as the International Amateur Athletic Federation, to follow the lead shown by their counterparts in football and swimming, and vote to cancel South Africa's membership.

A loaded voting system meant we needed more than a simple majority, but we sensed the opportunity might just arise when the Marquis of Exeter, a long-standing ally of South Africa who had ruled athletics for 30 years, announced his intention to step down as President.

Adriaan Paulen, of the Netherlands, emerged as a credible candidate, but, if he was to have any chance, he needed to bank Africa's votes. In a sport where we had long felt outgunned, at last we seemed to have some leverage.

African athletics was led by Lamine Diack of Senegal, and, despite his government's negative attitude towards the African Olympic boycott, he provided outstanding leadership and did the deal with Paulen: Lamine would bring all Africa's 84 votes to support him as President if he brought an equal number to expel South Africa.

All seemed well, but we faced a new problem. The 30th IAAF Congress in Montreal was being held during the first week of the Olympic Games, while the swimming and gymnastics were taking place, and before the athletics started.

Our predicament was that many of the African delegates to the IAAF had arrived in Canada with their respective Olympic teams; now that most of these teams had boycotted the Games and gone home, these people had nowhere to stay in a city where every hotel was full.

We had worked hard to do a deal with Paulen, but everything would be wasted if we could not ensure our delegates were able to attend the IAAF meeting.

In the end, we were rescued by Hassine Hamouda, a Tunisian working for Adidas, who somehow managed to find some rooms for our officials. Such acts of kindness invariably go unreported and unappreciated, but they enabled us to proceed and realise our goal.

The Congress assembled, Paulen was elected as President and the expulsion of South Africa became the subject of a fierce debate, with the Marquis of Exeter and his supporters standing by their friends right to the bitter end.

Our strategy was being directed by Lamine and Jean-Claude Ganga, and, as the arguments raged from the podium, I floated around the hall, scurrying between rows of delegates, arranging the order of our speakers in such a way that their words carried the greatest impact.

We alternated English speakers with French speakers to convey universality, and we found our hero in Wajid Ali, a widely respected official from Pakistan, an IOC member and married to a South African, who delivered a wonderful, rousing speech.

"Well spoken, Wajid, you really steamrollered the opposition," I told him that day in Montreal, and, every time I have met him ever since, we recall his performance with pleasure.

The vote was eventually taken, and the South Africans were expelled from the IAAF, albeit by a narrow margin. A great cheer rose from around the hall, hailing a highly significant victory for the anti-apartheid sports movement.

Later that evening, Jean-Claude Ganga and I were celebrating with a drink in the bar when we were approached by the ageing, limping figure of the Marquis of Exeter, himself.

The IAAF Congress had presented him with a spectacular golden trophy as a sign of in appreciation for his long years of service to the sport, and he clearly had something to tell us. We greeted him with respect, and smiled courteously.

"You chaps," he said. "You might have got South Africa expelled, but do you know where the gold in this trophy came from?"

This was obviously a rhetorical question, so we said nothing and waited for the answer.

"South Africa!" he barked, and left.

We allowed the Marquis to have the last word, but the enduring effect of a frenetic ten days in Montreal was to seriously weaken and irrevocably damage the crumbling fortress of apartheid sport.

The African boycott of the Olympic Games was painful in many respects, but it focussed world attention on South Africa's racial policies and it successfully isolated New Zealand.

Equally, the hat trick of successes at FIFA, FINA and the IAAF essentially completed the isolation of South African teams from mainstream international sport.

Of course, the country did retain membership of international federations in sports like fencing, gymnastics, rowing and canoeing, where the lack of African representation gave us little influence, but the global protest was loud and clear.

Before Montreal, SANROC was regarded as a pressure group with not much real clout. After Montreal, we were taken seriously.

Some observers branded us as spoilsports for disrupting the Olympic Games; others hailed our success in undermining apartheid.

For our part, we returned to London, inspired to keep fighting for the cause. Publicity brought more requests for interviews, more invitations to appear on television and a series of opportunities to address all kinds of public meetings.

Quietly, I felt we were starting to win the argument.

WINNING THE ARGUMENT

Thursday August 5th, 1976

The *Daily Mail* has had another crack at SANROC in this morning's edition. Once again, we are cast as Communist puppets who use a political agenda to sabotage international sport.

We never thought our role in facilitating the African boycott of the Olympic Games in Montreal would exactly endear us to the right-wing media in Britain, but their coverage has been vicious. A *Daily Mail* journalist approached us in Montreal and seemed quite supportive, but he was just gathering personal information about each of us, preparing what amounts to a hatchet job.

They have also criticised one of our main sources of funding, the International Defence and Aid Fund, and they have attacked the freehold owners of Chris de Broglio's hotel for allowing us to run the SANROC office in the basement: they say we are not entitled to do so in terms of the lease. It seems very petty.

In any case, nobody likes to be attacked in the press, and I can sense some people are starting to get jittery.

Even our local newspaper in Chingford, Essex has joined the chorus, and I can't pretend that headlines such as 'Local teacher sabotages Olympics' are not embarrassing for me.

At least, my local Labour Party councillor in Chingford, Peter Leyton, has been extremely supportive and helpful. Hopefully, this media storm will blow over before too long.

Monday August 16th, 1976

At an Anti-Apartheid Movement meeting in London, someone came up to me and asked how many staff SANROC employs. I hadn't met him before, so I was evasive. Dennis Brutus's warning all those years ago, that London is full of spies, still rings in my ears.

In fact, of course, we don't employ anyone and we get by on annual donations totalling around £12 000.

This man persisted, enquiring whether our headquarters are in a central London office block. I nodded vaguely.

He asked: "Do you take two or three floors of office space?"

I almost laughed out loud.

Our involvement at the Olympics in Montreal seems to have created the impression, around the world and also in South Africa, that we are some kind of vast organisation with a head office in London, and satellite offices around the world.

In reality, we are a handful of part-time volunteers working out of a borrowed room in the basement of a hotel. Nonetheless, if your cause is just, the people will hear.

Wednesday September 15th, 1976

Chris de Broglio and I have discussed our funding arrangements and everything seems to be settled again.

Canon John Collins, of the International Defence and Aid Fund (IDAF), told us they cannot afford the negative publicity and would no longer be able to channel funding to SANROC.

Instead, he suggested the money from the Swedish International Development Aid Agency (SIDA), would be routed to us via the Swedish Sports Confederation. Otherwise, we seem to have survived our bout of notoriety.

This 'stock-taking' has impressed on me once again the extent to which we are assisted by so many people around the world. These people go out of their way to help, not for any personal gain, just because they believe in what we are doing.

Helen McCue works for an anti-apartheid group in Sydney, and is instrumental in channelling a regular donation from the Australian Government Aid Agency.

We also receive funding from the Canadian government, organised by Ann Hillmer, a committed lady who works in the sports section of the Foreign Ministry.

Hans Skaset is another stalwart. Chairman of the Norwegian Sports

Federation, he helps to divert funds from the Ministry of Culture.

SIDA has also been fantastically generous. We deal with its southern Africa representative, Ernst Michanik, and his daughter, Lisbeth. In fact, both have become close friends of mine. Stig Hedlund, from the Swedish Sports Confederation, has been another great supporter of our cause.

Judge a man by his friends, wrote WB Yeats. Well, SANROC is extremely happy to be judged by our friends.

It's strange.

Our opponents are resolutely convinced we are funded from the Soviet Union and Eastern Europe, when those nations give us nothing but occasional air tickets when we visit them. In reality, our money comes mainly from Canada, Australia, Norway and Sweden.

Wednesday March 9th, 1977

The grapevine suggests we will see positive developments at the Commonwealth Heads of Government Meeting in June. CHOGM, as it's popularly known, will be held in London.

This is encouraging.

It seems as though the Canadian Prime Minister, Pierre Trudeau, is pressing for the meeting to take a united stand against apartheid sport, and so persuade the African countries to compete at next year's 1978 Commonwealth Games in Edmonton. He wants to avoid a Montreal-style boycott.

We are now working hard behind the scenes, preparing draft statements, finding the words that would satisfy the African nations on the one hand and countries like Britain and New Zealand on the other. As always, this is a delicate balancing act.

A Springbok rugby tour of New Zealand is looming in a few year's time, and a right-wing New Zealand Prime Minister has recently been elected after campaigning in favour of the rugby tour, saying, "I will personally attend the Test matches."

As usual, Jeremy Pope, legal adviser at the Commonwealth Secretariat and a determined and exceptionally bright supporter of our cause, is playing an important role in preparing a draft document for the attention of Commonwealth Secretary-General Sridath Ramphal.

Wednesday June 15th, 1977

At CHOGM meetings, it has become traditional for Heads of Government to take a day out of their formal meetings, and escape to a more relaxed environment. This time, they have escaped from London and decamped to Gleneagles in Scotland.

In these beautiful surroundings, they have finally approved a comprehensive declaration on apartheid sport.

We have received a document entitled the Commonwealth Statement on Apartheid in Sport, although it is already being called the Gleneagles Agreement. It's pretty emphatic.

"Apartheid in sport, as in other fields, is an abomination," it declares unequivocally, adding that sporting contact with South Africa represents tacit approval of apartheid.

The statement then concludes: "The Heads of Government specially welcomed the belief, unanimously expressed at their meeting, that there are unlikely to be future sporting contacts of any significance between Commonwealth countries, or their nationals, and South Africa while that country continues to pursue the detestable policy of apartheid.

"On that basis, and having regard to their commitments, they looked forward with satisfaction to the holding of the 1978 Commonwealth Games in Edmonton and to the continued strengthening of Commonwealth sport generally."

Some of our allies, notably Abraham Ordia and the Nigerian delegation, felt the wording could have been stronger, and there is no doubt that we would have preferred a firm commitment to stop all sporting contact with South Africa, but I believed we had reached a reasonable compromise. It was worthwhile.

Apparently Ramphal orchestrated the whole affair with a touch of genius. New Zealand's Muldoon was the likely sticking point. After considering the strengths and personal relationships of the various leaders, Ramphal mandated Jamaica's Prime Minister Michael Manley to tell Muldoon he had no option but to go along with the document. Manley chose to do this in the hotel bar.

At least, the Commonwealth has taken a stand together. In some ways, a noose has been placed around the neck of apartheid sport. Our challenge in the coming months and years is to sustain our campaigns and, tug by tug, to tighten that noose.

The Gleneagles Agreement is a huge achievement for us. For the first time an international governmental organisation has signed up to our cause.

Wednesday November 9th, 1977

We're winning minds at the United Nations.

The first stage of our campaign was to secure South Africa's expulsion from the major sports codes, such as football, athletics and swimming. We achieved that goal and also organised a major act of protest, the African boycott of the Olympics.

Now, we have entered a new phase, broadening the campaign to exclude South Africa from other federations and to discourage all foreign athletes from competing in South Africa. We believe the United Nations is the place to drive this process.

Enuga Reddy has been fantastic. He is an Indian national who heads the UN Centre against Apartheid, and has been largely responsible for driving this entire process. He has organised and addressed many international conferences and seminars on apartheid, always going the extra mile to expose the illegality of the regime.

Thursday April 1st, 1978

Today, I have started working full-time at SANROC.

It is not an easy decision to leave the teaching profession after 20 years, but my growing commitment to SANROC has made it harder and harder for me to do fulfil my responsibilities as Deputy Head at the Gwyn Jones School in Leytonstone, East London. I have held that position for three years, and was sorry to resign and leave the staff and pupils.

The Executive Board of SANROC has been sympathetic to my situation and, with funding in place, they suggested that I should become the first full-time official of the organisation.

We have agreed a reasonable salary package, even though the loss of certain benefits and pension schemes means we will be financially worse off than when I was teaching.

Helga has accepted the situation. She has been in London for five months now, and life is not easy, but she understands what my work at SANROC means to me, and she is prepared to make the necessary sacrifices. I will make it up to her one day.

In any case, I have taken a close look at our situation and, cutting back here and there, I'm sure we will get by.

Friday April 7th, 1978

Another week, another meeting, another statement.

The European Ministers of Sport have gathered in London and issued a statement, which, in paragraph six, reads: "The Ministers emphasise their opposition to any discrimination in sport, which is based on race, religion, politics or any other criterion in contradiction to the Olympic Charter, and draw the attention of the governing bodies of sport to the International Declaration against Apartheid in Sports, adopted by the United Nations."

That's OK. Somebody said the communiqué should mention South Africa by name, but the use of the word 'apartheid' doesn't leave too much room for misunderstanding.

It's another solid statement of intent, another distinct step, another discernible drip in our drip, drip, drip campaign.

There are times when I wonder whether these declarations and conventions really add up to very much, whether government officials draft them, issue them, file them and forget them.

Maybe that happens, yet the relentless flow of international statements does sustain and increase pressure on the regime. We are opposed by a ruthless, racist government fuelled by a zealous sense of self-preservation and huge mineral wealth.

Nobody said the contest would be easy.

It isn't.

Who must I telephone tomorrow?

Thursday July 20th, 1978

I have been working as a consultant to the United Nations Centre Against Apartheid in New York City for the past three months, and will be returning to humdrum London next week.

It has been an incredibly stimulating period of my life. Many people are cynical about this organisation, deriding it as a talking shop that achieves little, but that is unfair on the thousands of good people here who work tirelessly to improve lives.

My accreditation gives me access to all areas and, as I walk around the buildings, I enjoy the sense of a melting pot of so many nationalities and cultures. The work has been mainly focussed on research and drafting statements, speeches and resolutions relating to the UN campaign against apartheid, but I have taken the opportunity to attend meetings on other issues, like the Middle East.

I have got to know most of the African delegates and their staff, and they have all treated me like a colleague. The Eastern Europeans are extremely friendly, and I have met Andrew Young, the current United States Ambassador to the UN.

Each evening, many representatives gather in an open area, known as the Delegates' Lounge, to chat about the day's events over a drink, and I always try to be there because it's a perfect time and place to meet influential people from different countries and diverse backgrounds.

One day, I might be talking to the Polish ambassador to the UN; the next day, I may be with a group of Canadians.

This secondment to the UN has worked well for SANROC because the UN has been paying my salary, saving us some money and easing our financial position. In fact, it seems the UN wants me to continue consulting to the Centre from London and that they will be prepared to pay me an annual grant for this work. I will use that as a subsidy, not a supplement, to my salary from SANROC.

There is talk they will ask me to spend another three months here next year. If so, I will eagerly book my flights.

Tuesday August 19th, 1980

Once again, I am spending the days preceding the Olympic Games in meetings with officials from various African countries. Four years ago in Montreal, I was urging them to boycott the Games, but, now, in Moscow, I am imploring them to stay and compete. The United States and their allies are boycotting the Olympics in protest at the Soviet invasion of Afghanistan, and several African countries are coming under pressure to comply.

"All I say is this," I tell the Africans. "The Eastern European countries have always offered us support and, now, in their time of need, we should show some solidarity to them. The Americans are not our friends. They have done nothing for us."

People are listening, and I am extremely confident that very few African countries will join the American-led boycott.

Wednesday October 15th, 1980

It was Enuga Reddy's idea. He suggested we should address the continuing problem of individual sportsmen and women travelling to compete in South Africa by creating a United Nations Register of International Sports Contacts with South Africa.

I liked the concept. It would be an exercise in public naming and shaming, and would serve as a strong deterrent.

Enuga pursued the idea, developed a plan and, this morning in New York, he has launched the so-called blacklist.

"We will compile a register of sportsmen and -women, sports administrators and others who flagrantly violate the sports boycott against South Africa," he said, in his capacity as Head of the UN Centre against Apartheid. "The register will then be made available to governments and organisations all over the world to facilitate action against collaborators with apartheid."

SANROC's role was to supply Enuga's office with an initial list of names and then regularly update the information. I have already sent the request to my SACOS friends in South Africa.

As usual, the Swedish government is the first to demonstrate support for our cause. They have declared that any person whose name appears on the UN register will not be allowed to compete in a sporting event on Swedish soil, without exceptions.

Wednesday December 17th, 1980

As an organisation, the Supreme Council for Sport in Africa has always been one of our most resolved and cooperative supporters, and we have always taken the trouble to attend their meetings and keep them involved and informed on our campaign.

Today I am in Freetown, Sierra Leone. It is almost midnight and I am working on the speech I am due to deliver to the SCSA meeting tomorrow afternoon. My primary aim is to challenge and expose recent attempts by the South African government to portray their sports structures as reformed, multiracial and deserving of recognition.

I will start by outlining how a few black athletes are being put in the window box of South African sport, elevated to veneer the apartheid policy with respectability and fool the world into thinking that the country offers equal opportunities in sport.

As usual in my speeches, I will try to support my statements with facts; so I will list the racial laws that remain on the statute book and prevent non-racial sport from taking place, quoting the Minister of Sport and Recreation in Parliament when he confirmed the laws apply to sport as they do to everything else.

I will also refer to a newspaper cutting from the South African *Sunday Times*, telling how a talented black athlete was selected to compete at the national provincial athletics championships, and was hailed as a prime example of multiracial sport.

However, the evening after his race, he was left alone in his hotel room because all his white teammates went to see a film at a cinema from which black people were barred.

"It is clear," I will tell them, "that no normal sport is possible in an abnormal society. You cannot separate the event from the society in which it is staged. Recent changes in South African sport are, therefore, only cosmetic. They will never be fundamental until the apartheid laws are revoked.

"So, it is of the utmost importance that Africa, together with her international allies in the anti-apartheid movement, take immediate action to counter this apartheid manoeuvre."

As I scanned the words, I kept in mind the advice of Ydnekatcheou Tessema, the President of the Confederation of African Football, who always reminds me to omit the names of those few African countries, such as Ivory Coast, Malawi and Senegal, which are sometimes ambivalent in their approach to South Africa.

I re-read the speech, just to check everything is accurate and correct. It looks all right. Now, I need some sleep.

Thursday June 25th, 1981

While the rest of the sporting world has confronted the issue and isolated the injustice of apartheid sport, rugby union has carried on blissfully regardless of international opinion.

Administrators and players throughout the game seem totally oblivious to the fact their continued contact with South Africa, both in hosting the Springboks and sending teams to the republic, serves to bolster and encourage the apartheid regime.

"We don't mix sport with politics," they claim, overlooking the fact that it is their celebrated 'friends', the white South African rugby elite, who bring politics into the game by specifically denying facilities and opportunity to their black compatriots.

"Why can't we have contact with South Africa when we play many countries with dubious political systems," they ask, wilfully ignoring the reality that, uniquely, apartheid denies equal sporting opportunities to people because they are black.

Time and again, over the past few years, I have requested meetings with representatives of the International Rugby Board and the Rugby Football Union in London to make these points, maybe to bring rugby in line with mainstream world opinion.

More often than not, I don't even receive the courtesy of a reply. Its head buried deep in the sand, rugby stubbornly clings to its precious friendships and turns a blind eye to evil.

Beyond the support of a few individuals like John Taylor, of Wales, and Bob Burgess, of New Zealand, we have found it difficult to gain a foothold in a code with no significant representation or presence from Asian, Eastern European or African countries.

In 1980, the South African Springboks played no fewer than nine officially recognised international Test matches: two against the Jaguars, a composite touring side, four against the British Lions, two on tour to South America and one against France in Pretoria.

This year, the Irish team has already toured South Africa, playing Tests in Cape Town and Durban, and now the Springboks are in the midst of a full tour to New Zealand.

Amid our successes in other codes and at the Olympics, our inability to isolate South African rugby is depressing; and it's made worse by the knowledge that, if they could select one sport to keep playing, the moguls of apartheid would choose rugby.

Could we have done any more?

Only two years ago, in 1979, I travelled up and down New Zealand, making a series of speeches about apartheid in sport, and I gradually sensed a strong groundswell opinion against maintaining their long-standing rugby links with South Africa.

I met many committed men, like Tom Newnham, the writer and activist in Auckland, Trevor Richards, who established the Halt All Racist Tours (HART) organisation, and John Minto, who is leading the demonstrations during the current tour.

David Wickham and Chris Laidlaw, the former All Black scrumhalf, were others who were prepared to risk criticism and take a moral stand in refusing to play with apartheid.

However, notwithstanding the impassioned debate dividing his country down the middle, Prime Minister Robert Muldoon remained absolutely determined that the Springboks should be invited to tour New Zealand during June and July, 1981.

We have maintained close links with HART, offering support where possible, and major public demonstrations have been held at every match and every hotel where the Springboks stay. The game in Hamilton was cancelled before it could start.

Sadly, the tour is proceeding.

Tuesday February 9th, 1982

Last night was not much fun at our house in Chingford, an ordinary terraced home in a quiet suburb east of London.

I had spent the evening as a studio guest at LBC radio, taking part in a phone-in programme about rugby and isolation of South African sport. One caller nearly became abusive, but 80 percent of the calls were extremely supportive, as they usually are.

It was past ten o'clock by the time I got home, and I had just settled into an armchair to watch the television news when we were startled by the deafening sound of shattering glass.

Helga was sitting on the opposite side of the room, and we instinctively took cover, eventually looking up to discover a large spiked stone had been hurled through our front window.

The object had effectively been stopped in its flight by the thick, heavy curtains we had bought for the living room. If they had not been drawn, there is no doubt that either Helga or I would have been seriously injured. We had had a lucky escape.

"Are you all right," my wife asked.

"Yes, I'm fine," I replied. "Not even a cut."

Neither of us slept well, even though our friendly neighbours had come out and helped us board up the window for the night.

This morning, we reported the incident to the police. They didn't seem overly concerned. "Probably just a couple of kids," the constable said. We're not so sure, but life goes on.

Thursday April 8th, 1982

There are bullet marks on the bedroom wall.

Last night, somebody stood in the street and fired a birdshot gun at our first-floor bedroom window. Once again someone was looking after us, and neither Helga nor I were hurt, but this second attack on our home is unsettling and alarming.

We called the police again, and even showed them one of the bullets that we found on the bedroom floor, but they did not seem very excited or optimistic about finding the culprit.

"Sam, we have to move," Helga said.

My nature is to dig my heels in whenever I am opposed, but, in this instance, I realise my wife is right. We have been lucky twice in the space of two months, but whoever is trying to harm us only needs to be lucky once. We must leave Chingford.

"Yes, dear," I said, "but where do we go?"

We discussed the options, and have decided to start looking in north London because we have friends in places like Hampstead, Camden and Islington, exiled South Africans and members of the anti-apartheid and Labour Party movements.

It would clearly have to be a flat, preferably above the first floor with reasonable security; and, I told the estate agents, we had to have a solid lock-up garage for the car.

Chris de Broglio is being very helpful during this difficult period, and we have also been greatly supported by Peter Hain, a leading member of the anti-apartheid movement and the man who led the protests against the 1969/70 Springbok tour of Britain.

Monday April 19th, 1982

Personal security has become an issue. It's in my head. Suddenly, any person walking towards me starts to look like an assailant and every situation begins to feel dangerous.

I had a meeting with a Parliamentary adviser in Westminster this morning, and just happened to mention the two attacks on our house. He claimed to have experience in such matters and urged me to start taking some straightforward precautions.

He said we should arrange a postal address, and, so far as possible, keep our physical address out of the public domain. He also told me to avoid walking alone at night, especially in dark alleys.

The two incidents have made me aware, but I am determined not to become paranoid about our security. Helga and I have always felt safe in London, and I don't want that to change just because a couple of thugs have tried to get us rattled.

They won't succeed.

Wednesday April 28th, 1982

Sir Edward Williams, Chief Justice of Queensland, approached us late last year. He is an Australian, so I was instinctively prepared to be as helpful as possible.

In his capacity as Chairman of the Organising Committee of this year's XII Commonwealth Games in Brisbane, Sir Edward wanted to make sure Australia's anti-apartheid credentials were sufficiently fortified to avoid any boycott of the Games.

I didn't think there would be a problem, but Sir Edward and I proposed that a meeting of the Commonwealth Games Federation (CGF) be held in London. This suggestion was welcomed both by Sir Alexander Ross, a

London-based New Zealander who is President of the CGF, and by Sridath Ramphal, Secretary-General of the Commonwealth, and they arranged today's meeting at Marlborough House.

It was a useful opportunity to keep everyone informed and on board, and it became clear the Games will not be disrupted. That is as it should be, because Australia has for many years been a sound supporter of the campaign against apartheid sport.

In 1971, soon after being elected as his country's first Labour Prime Minister in 33 years, Gough Whitlam effectively slammed the door on South African sport by introducing measures that ensured South Africans would not be permitted to play any team sports on Australian soil. No ifs and buts, he banned them.

This firm, uncompromising policy has been maintained by the conservative government of Malcolm Fraser.

So, Sir Edward has received the assurance he sought, and his Games will be a success. Australia deserves nothing less.

Sunday August 17th, 1982
Our lives seem to have settled down since the excitement at the start of the year. We have found a flat in Hampstead and, as long as there are no hitches, we'll move in September.

Helga and I have a clear purpose in our lives and, while there are moments of stress, we remain content in London. On a personal level, we feel surrounded by a strong circle of friends.

There are South African exiles, like Aziz Pahad, who has a flat in north London, and his brother Essop, who lives in Maida Vale.

We also see Jasmat Dhiraj on a regular basis, and the former tennis star is a member of the SANROC Executive; and we see Sylvester Stein, a former editor of *Drum* magazine and author of *Second Class Taxi*, a book banned in South Africa. Then, we have British friends. Jenny Hargreaves is a lecturer in sport at Roehampton College, but she still finds time to ensure our various activities are approved and supported by the broader Anti-Apartheid Movement in Britain and beyond. Ruth and Robert Browning also live in Hampstead. Ruth helps us with translation, and Robert is a Professor of Byzantium history at the University of London.

Bob Hughes and Mike Terry are other leading members of the AAM, who have become trusted friends. Robert Archer has written a well-received book on South Africa, and he often offers invaluable assistance at various conventions and conferences.

Tuesday February 8th, 1983

Our campaign lost a fine and brave man on New Year's Day with the passing of Canon John Collins, a canon at St Paul's Cathedral and the inspiration behind the International Defence and Aid Fund.

I attended his funeral in January, together with a close friend, Kader Asmal, and I also made sure that I could be present at his memorial service in the cathedral this afternoon.

Canon Collins was an important supporter of SANROC, not just because he arranged funding through the IDAF but also because he sincerely shared our passion for the cause.

His contribution to the wider liberation struggle was epic. Over a period of 25 years, Canon Collins and the IDAF smuggled more than £100 million into South Africa, primarily for the purpose of funding the legal defence of political activists and, if necessary, providing aid to their families while they were in prison.

In 1956, when the South African regime launched the first of its treason trials, he stepped forward to guarantee the legal costs and support for each of the 156 accused and their families.

People doubted how a priest could make such a commitment, but he proved as good as his word. He wrote to the newspapers, held protest meetings and art exhibitions, he even had Paul Robeson singing spirituals in the cathedral. Almost single-handedly, the untiring canon raised £170 000 and helped to sustain the defence in a trial that dragged on for four years before the last defendant was acquitted.

When the IDAF was officially banned in South Africa, under the Suppression of Communism Act, Collins instituted a system of legal firms using numbered trust accounts to channel money into South Africa and keep providing defence and aid.

He used to meet intermediaries in the Chapter House, or even in the deserted cathedral, whispering across the pews.

Father Trevor Huddleston will succeed Canon Collins as President of the IDAF, and it was appropriate that he should have given the address today. Oliver Tambo, exiled leader of the African National Congress, read the parable of the Good Samaritan.

If ever there was a Good Samaritan for South Africa, it was Canon John Collins. South Africans should respect both his memory and the enormous contribution of his wife, Diana.

Friday June 9th, 1983

Soon after one o'clock in the morning, it became clear that Margaret Thatcher and the Conservatives had won the General Election by a comfortable majority, securing a second term.

I had some respect for her as a politician, but her strategy of trying to influence South Africa by maintaining contact with Pretoria contrasted strongly with our policy of isolation.

There were times when her statements defied logic. One day, she stands up in the House of Commons and condemns a handful of anti-apartheid protesters for disrupting a sports event in London where South Africans have been allowed to compete.

Then, when black professional footballers are racially abused at First Division matches, she says nothing at all.

This Prime Minister is not a product of the establishment, but her perspective seems to reflect the long-standing sympathy for white South Africa among England's ruling classes.

Perhaps the grandees of the Gentlemen's clubs on Pall Mall still regard South Africa as a 'bastion of civilisation' in an otherwise dark, mysterious and unfathomable continent.

Maybe they keep in mind South Africa's strategic significance, and reach the unspoken conclusion that, while apartheid is far from acceptable, it remains preferable to Communism.

Could this explain why Britain appears so hesitant to condemn the South African government, so resolved not to impose economic sanctions on Pretoria and generally be so soft on apartheid?

I don't know. What I do know is that, in our campaign, we can expect no favours from Mrs Thatcher's government.

Monday November 21st, 1983

Sadly, the latest UN register includes the names of 14 West Indian cricketers who were lured to South Africa earlier this year, and will shortly be returning for the second leg of their tour.

The South African Cricket Union (SACU) began recruiting rebel tours to South Africa in 1981, and their lucrative contracts have too often been accepted by generally poorly paid cricketers. An English XI, led by Graham Gooch, has been followed by a Sri Lankan group and now the West Indians, captained by Lawrence Rowe.

However, anti-apartheid feelings run high in the Caribbean, and we have been encouraged by the attitudes of perhaps the two most prominent West Indians cricketers of recent times.

Viv Richards was approached by SACU, but turned them down flat. Clive Lloyd declined an invitation to meet South African officials in Sharjah, and publicly declared that all the gold in South Africa would not buy his conscience. Happily, money doesn't buy everyone.

Wednesday March 14th, 1984

We hear rumours all the time in the office, originating either from South Africa or from our various contacts around the world. If they all turned out to be true, our lives would be extremely exciting.

This one seems hard to believe. The name Zola Budd crossed our desk earlier in the month when we heard that an impish Afrikaans girl from Bloemfontein had produced an amazing time of 15 minutes 1,83 seconds for the 5 000m, running barefoot, seven seconds faster than the existing world record held by Mary Decker, of the USA.

Since South Africa is suspended from the IAAF, the new world record has not been officially recognised.

In any case, the story now runs that Zola Budd has a British grandfather and will apply for UK citizenship in time to compete for Britain at this year's Olympic Games in Los Angeles.

"Impossible," we said.

Saturday March 24th, 1984

Zola Budd arrives at Heathrow airport, flanked by representatives of the

Daily Mail and her ambitious father, Frank. She says she wants to run for Britain. Fiction has become fact.

Tuesday April 3rd, 1984

Today, we received the least surprising news of the year. Budd's application for British citizenship has been approved in record time and, settled in Guildford, she is now preparing to claim her place in the British Olympic team for Los Angeles.

I feel angry, but also sad.

This innocent teenager is being used by a British newspaper to boost circulation, by the pariah apartheid regime to gain some reflected glory and by a country desperate for medals. In this sorry saga, Budd is emerging as the biggest victim of all.

I find myself in an awkward position because I feel SANROC must unequivocally condemn what amounts to a South African star athlete running under a flag of convenience, but I am also reluctant for us to look like bullies harassing a naïve teenager.

When a reporter contacted me this afternoon and asked for my comment, I'm not sure I got the balance right.

"Zola Budd is most certainly an agent for apartheid," I told him frankly. "It's sickening to see Britain accepting her into their national team. This shows British sympathy for apartheid."

This is not a personal issue. It is a question of Britain being prepared to see this athlete deployed to undermine the campaign to end apartheid in sport. I hope my remarks reflect this plain reality when they appear in print tomorrow morning. Of course, most likely, I will be misquoted.

Thursday August 10th, 1984

Today's final of the women's 3 000m at the 1984 Olympic Games was eagerly billed as the showdown between Budd, the 'British' barefoot phenomenon, and Decker, the American darling prematurely being billed as the 'star' of the whole Games and expected to earn a fortune in subsequent endorsements.

It ends in tears, for almost everyone.

The two athletes tangled with each other after 1 700 metres. Decker fell

For many years, SANROC operated out of a room located in the basement of a London hotel, owned by Chris de Broglio. It may not have been glamorous, but it was adequate.

I returned to South Africa in 1991 and was reunited with my family.

Krish Naidoo led the highly successful National Sports Congress demonstration against the rebel English cricket tour in 1990, and helped create the conditions where unity in South African sport could be achieved.

The arrival in South Africa of a high-level IOC delegation gave impetus to what was always going to be a difficult and drawn-out unity process in South African sport. I greeted the group in Johannesburg with ANC leaders Oliver Tambo, with the walking stick, and Nelson Mandela. Mluleki George, President of the National Sports Congress, is standing on the right in the front row.

SOUTH AFRICAN OLYMPIC NEWS

SOUTH AFRICA

APRIL 1992

THE NEWSLETTER OF THE NATIONAL OLYMPIC COMMITTEE OF SOUTH AFRICA

SOUTH AFRICA WARMLY WELCOMED

congratulate the South African national Olympic committee. Now it is fully recognised by the international Olympic Committee," said IOC president His Excellency Mr Juan Antonio Samaranch, Marquis de Samaranch.

After more than three decades of isolation, South Africa, expelled in 1970 because of apartheid, has been admitted to the Olympic Movement. This has followed the abolition by the South African government of the last race laws which prevented the local national Olympic body from completely respecting the Olympic Charter.

handing to the National Olympic Committee of South Africa president, Mr Sam Ramsamy, the letter according full recognition.

The speech by the IOC president ended the day's proceedings on 9 July 1991, during which the South African delegation, led by Mr Ramsamy, had been received by the Apartheid and Olympism Commission under Mr Kéba Mbaye, IOC Vice-President from Senegal.

Earlier, South Africa was granted recognition subject to several conditions, including respect of Charter and normalisation of relations with continental sports organisations. Since then, NOCSA has assisted in unifying sports bodies in South Africa on a non-racial basis, and many federations have achieved such a merger.

"It's very important to us," declared Mr Ramsamy. "We wanted this recognition. It will help us not to worry about colour but instead to concentrate on the fact that we're all South Africans. We now have firmer control over Olympic sports in South Africa, and that will also have an effect on the non-Olympic sports."

The NOCSA president also stressed that "unity and non-racialism are meaningless if there is not going to be total and adequate participation of the disadvantaged sectors." Mr Ramsamy added, "The development of integrated sport will be served by the Republic's participation in international sport from which it has been isolated for two decades."

For Mr Jean-Claude Ganga, IOC member in the Congo, Association of Africa President and member of the Apartheid and Olympism Commission, it was "a victory for justice, as one can now say that within sport in South Africa, all men are equal whatever their colour. It is for this that we have been fighting for the past 23 years."

This official recognition, which brought to 167 the number of NOCs recognised by the IOC, puts an end to the ostracism respected by the majority of international sports federations.

His Excellency Mr Juan Antonio Samaranch, Marquis de Samaranch (right) congratulates Mr Sam Ramsamy on South Africa's admission to the Olympic family on 9 July 1991.

The most significant moment of the transition occurred on July 9th, 1991, when the National Olympic Committee of South Africa (NOCSA) was formally recognised by the IOC, represented by the IOC President, Juan Antonio Samaranch.

The IOC President visited South Africa and is here in discussion with Barbara Masekela, now the South African Ambassador in Washington, DC, and, to the right, Dr Ali Bacher, the dynamic former Managing Director of the United Cricket Board of South Africa and a close friend.

I first met Thabo Mbeki in London, when I was working for SANROC and he was operating within the ANC in exile. We have remained close ever since, and are seen here in conversation at Randjiesfontein, at the opening match of the West Indies cricket tour to South Africa in 1993.

and was carried away in the arms of her boyfriend, crying hysterically and angrily blaming Budd for the collision.

Budd looked lost and bewildered as the crowd start to hiss and boo her. A long way from home in Bloemfontein, bleeding and weeping, she finished an anonymous, agonised seventh. She was initially disqualified for cutting in on Decker, but later unanimously reinstated by the jury of appeal.

I watched this unbelievable sequence of events unfold from my seat in the stand at the Coliseum in Los Angeles, aghast, exchanging glances of amazement with Ismail Bhamjee, President of the Botswana National Olympic Committee, who was sitting nearby.

This saga has reflected badly on everyone involved: on Budd's advisers and the *Daily Mail* who pushed her too far, on Britain and British athletics who allowed the tale to unfold… and two athletes were left in tears of despair beside the Olympic track.

Sunday July 7th, 1985

It has been an extremely hot summer's day in London, and I have spent the afternoon at the All England Lawn Tennis and Croquet Club watching an unseeded 17-year-old German called Boris Becker play Kevin Curren in the Wimbledon men's singles final.

Curren is a South African, based in Texas. He defeated John McEnroe in the quarterfinal, and then overwhelmed Jimmy Connors in the semifinal for the loss of only five games. He actually comes from Durban, my home town.

Even so, I wanted him to lose because, if he had won the title, through no fault of his own, his success would have been trumpeted as a vindication of the status quo in South Africa.

Fortunately, Becker was too powerful. The German won the first set 6-3 and, even though the big-serving Curren levelled by winning a second set tiebreak, Becker won the next two sets, 7-6, 6-4 and became the youngest ever men's champion. I am relieved now and, on a purely personal level, just a little sad for Curren. He had been the favourite, and lost.

Friday July 12th, 1985

I received a telephone call around three o'clock this morning in London, just after lunch in Wellington, New Zealand.

The conversation lasted only a few minutes, after which Helga turned to me and blearily asked what was wrong.

"Not much, dear," I said. "The lawyers in New Zealand need NZ$1 million by this afternoon.

"What are we going to do," she asked, now sitting up, wide awake and alert to the crisis on the other side of the world.

"Well, we may have to use the flat as collateral," I said.

Silence.

"OK," she whispered, and we both went back to sleep.

The following situation had unfolded. The New Zealand rugby team were scheduled to tour South Africa in 1985, and we had sent our representative, the Reverend Arnold Stofile, to New Zealand to try and dissuade officials and players from going ahead.

He worked hard and effectively, but the rugby authorities were determined to proceed and, upon his return to South Africa, he was promptly thrown into prison, indicating the degree of collusion that existed between Muldoon's New Zealand and apartheid South Africa.

As a last resort, two club players in Auckland, Philip Recordon and Patrick Finnegan, used their legal knowledge to bring a court action against the New Zealand Rugby Union (NZRFU) on the grounds that they were acting contrary to its rules and constitution by accepting an invitation to tour South Africa.

The NZRFU constitution states that the Union must act in the best interests of the game and the two players claimed that they had a contract with the NZRFU that they were entitled to enforce.

The case was initially struck out by Chief Justice, Sir Ronald Davison on the basis that Recordon and Finnigan were not of proper standing as members of the NZRFU. However, this ruling was in part overturned by the Court of Appeal and the case went to the High Court in Wellington to be heard by Mr Justice Casey.

Ted Thomas, a Queen's Counsel who was later a Court of Appeal Judge, headed the legal team. Jeremy Pope had helped to prepare the case and spoke to Ted every day, suggesting that he ask for an interim order to prevent the team from travelling on the following Monday.

However, this morning (London time) he told Jeremy that he could not apply, as it would bankrupt his clients. He had spoken to the NZRFU lawyers and they wanted a copper-bottom guarantee for $1 million.

The team would be leaving in three days' time, but the court would continue to hear the case through the weekend. Jeremy asked Ted to hold fire and not to abandon the idea of the interim order. "Just give me twelve hours and let me see what I can do," he said. Ted agreed.

It was at this point that Jeremy called me at three this morning, asking where we could find NZ$1 million in 12 hours.

My first thought was to approach the IDAF, so Jeremy and I called Father Trevor Huddleston and arranged to see him at his church, St James' in Piccadilly, at 10 o'clock this morning.

Trevor had been unwell, and only recently come out of hospital, but he greeted us cheerfully, offering tea and cake.

I asked him how he was feeling.

"Oh, I'm OK," he said, wistfully. "I told God I am not ready to go upstairs yet. I want to see the end of apartheid first." Coming to the point, he continued: "I gather you have a problem."

We explained our dilemma in New Zealand.

"I'm afraid we can't use the resources of the Defence and Aid Fund for something like that, but we will have to find a way," he said, going on to suggest I contact Ernst Michanik in Stockholm.

I drove straight home and called Ernst, our contact at the Swedish International Development Aid Agency, but he replied that SIDA, like the IDAF, could not make such a donation, up front at least.

"Well, Sam," Jeremy said. "There's only one solution that I can see, and that's for you to offer your Hampstead flat as a guarantee, but that's obviously a gamble for you and Helga and there's no certainty that the two players will win the case. This is making new law."

I felt it needed to be done. We needed to stop the tour, and Helga agreed with me.

It all seemed pretty hairy, but Ted Thomas — more than surprised at the speed with which all this had been accomplished — said he would apply for the interim injunction first thing on Saturday morning.

If it is physically possible to go to sleep while holding one's breath, that is exactly what I achieved that night.

Saturday July 13th, 1985
It's five o'clock in the morning in London, mid-afternoon in New Zealand, and the telephone is ringing again. I recognise Ted Thomas's voice immediately and he tells me that Mr Justice Casey has just granted the interim injunction against the tour. It is the lead item on the BBC World Service news bulletins. Jeremy and I can hardly believe we have managed to pull this off.

Thursday July 18th, 1985
I hear Ces Blazey, chairman of the NZRFU Council, interviewed on the radio and he says the NZRFU has cancelled all plans for a tour to South Africa, but adds there is now talk of the All Blacks wanting to tour as individuals, without the consent of their union.

Sunday July 21st, 1985
South Africa is first on the BBC TV news tonight. After protests in townships near Johannesburg and Cape Town, the State President, PW Botha, has declared a State of Emergency.

Tuesday July 23rd, 1985
We are told the New Zealand rugby players have met to discuss their options and finally decided to stay at home.

Their South African tour is cancelled. We have won.

At long last, it seems as if the sport of rugby union has been dragged, literally kicking and screaming through the courts, to join the rest of the sporting world in isolating apartheid. I called Father Huddleston this evening to inform him of the final cancellation. During our discussion, he mentioned that I would not have had to worry about offering our flat as collateral.

"If Ernst had not come through for you," he told me, "I would have raised the cash myself. In any case, I was always confident that we would get the right result in New Zealand."

Tuesday December 10th, 1985
Several months of hard work comes to fruition with news that the General Assembly of the United Nations has ratified another strong International Convention against apartheid in sports.

The convention comprises 22 articles, including agreement that 'States Parties' shall not permit sports contact with a country practising apartheid and shall take appropriate action to ensure that their bodies, teams and individuals do not have such contact.

It details the actions to be taken against sports bodies, teams and individuals that participate 'in sports activities in a country practising apartheid': these include the withholding of funding, the restriction of access to national sports facilities, the denial or even withdrawal of national honours and the denial of official receptions to such teams or individual sportsmen and -women.

The convention also provides for the institution of a 15-person Commission against Apartheid in Sports, to oversee implementation of the agreement and to punish flagrant breaches. I quickly scan the text of the declaration, which has arrived at our office by fax, and it looks emphatic and strong. When the day comes that apartheid falls, nobody will be able to say the UN sat on its collective hands and did nothing.

Tuesday December 10th, 1985

Next year's planned British Lions tour to South Africa was cancelled this morning. South African rugby is firmly isolated now.

Thursday April 24th, 1986

Maybe this was inevitable. We hear that 30 leading New Zealand rugby players have arrived in South Africa, calling themselves the Cavaliers and planning to play four Tests against the Springboks in an unofficial and unauthorised 12-match tour.

After rebel cricket tours (an Australian squad have recently been touring South Africa), we have a rebel rugby tour. Huge tax breaks for the nominal sponsors means these grotesque ventures are being funded by the South African government.

Tuesday June 10th, 1986

It's now clear that no fewer than 32 countries, from Africa, Asia and the Caribbean, will boycott this year's XIII Commonwealth Games in Edinburgh. Only 26 nations are planning to attend.

The split has been prompted by Britain's refusal to impose sanctions against South Africa. Margaret Thatcher made her stand clear at a Commonwealth Heads of Government meeting in Lusaka, Zambia, thereby precipitating the boycott. Indeed, Britain's intransigent attitude prompted Major General Henry Adefope, the Nigerian Foreign Minister, to announce his government would immediately retaliate by nationalising the British Petroleum operation in Nigeria.

Right-wing British newspapers have accused countries like Nigeria of being so wedded to a political agenda that they never had any intention of competing in Edinburgh.

This is nonsense. The Nigerians have already spent more than US$ 1 million preparing their athletes for the Games.

Sunday July 13th, 1986

Zola Budd and Annette Cowley, a South African swimmer claiming to be British, have today been withdrawn from the English team to compete at the Commonwealth Games in Edinburgh. Another long SANROC campaign has yielded a positive result.

We have simply pointed out that neither Budd nor Cowley had spent the legally required number of days in Britain to sustain their qualification to compete in the Games. Budd was effectively based in South Africa, and Cowley spent most of her time in the United States. Neither could be described as resident in the UK.

Our opponents repeatedly claim we are bullying these young girls, but this has never been personal. The fact is that high-profile South African athletes competing on the international stage under a flag of convenience represent a coup for apartheid.

Within our continuing campaign to isolate and eventually overcome apartheid in sport, we cannot stand by and allow such blatant abuses to go unchallenged; in the past few months, we have argued our case in a calm and rational manner.

This afternoon, I telephoned Sharad Rao, legal adviser to the Commonwealth Games Federation, and Jeremy Pope to thank them for their efforts in preparing our case.

In fact, people have been complaining that Jeremy spends too much time assisting SANROC, but the situation is under control. The Secretary-General of the Commonwealth, Sir Sridath Ramphal, is a strong supporter of our cause, and he has simply asked Jeremy to be more discreet in his anti-apartheid activities.

Kader Asmal, a South African exile based in Ireland, has also played an important role in drawing up the legal documents relating to Budd and Cowley. This has been a team effort.

Tuesday July 15th, 1986

The controversy over Budd and Cowley is still rumbling on, with a few newspapers casting them as innocent victims and claiming we have attacked them just because they are white.

In a series of media interviews this afternoon, I have tried to set the record straight and make two points clear.

First, even their supporters accept that both Budd and Cowley would have eased the situation if they had publicly condemned the system of apartheid. Neither has been willing to do so.

Second, their case is often compared to that of Sidney Maree, a black South African middle-distance runner who settled in the USA and has been competing under the American flag. Critics ask why we pursue Budd, and leave Maree alone.

The difference is simple.

Our opposition to Budd lies in the fact that, by steadfastly refusing to denounce apartheid, she has allowed herself to become generally portrayed as a symbol of the system, and she has been unashamedly hailed as such inside South Africa.

She may merit some sympathy on a personal level, but her achievements, notably winning World Cross Country Championship titles in 1985 and 1986, have been celebrated as the triumphs of a South African who has defied international isolation.

This has never been the case with Maree. In fact, he came to see me while I was working at the United Nations in New York and, having travelled from his home in Pennsylvania, he told me how he was committed to the liberation struggle and would have nothing to do with South Africa until apartheid was ended.

He said he would occasionally go home to visit his family in the township of Atteridgeville, near Pretoria, but that he would never say or do anything to create the impression that he was any kind of boycott-busting sporting ambassador.

I hope that is clear now. We'll have to see how my comments are reflected in the newspapers. I'm not optimistic.

Monday February 9th, 1987

For many years, SANROC has been able to rely on the support of several high-profile English footballers, and four of them turned up to attend one of our functions at Chris de Broglio's hotel this evening.

In fact, far from showing any reluctance, Garth Crooks and Chris Houghton, both of Spurs, Brian Stein, of Luton Town, (whose father Isaiah was actually a member of the SANROC Executive) and Mark Hughes, of Manchester United, all told me they wanted to do more to express their support for our struggle.

"Well, we have to be careful," I told them. "It's wonderful that you come to these functions and we will continue to use your names in various publications and press releases.

"But I don't think you should put yourselves in the front line by giving radio and television interviews on the subject."

They seemed disappointed.

"If you do that," I continued, "certain people may start trying to victimise you and make your lives difficult, and that could affect your form and your careers. We don't want that to happen."

We spoke for a while, and they seemed to understand.

Thursday September 15th, 1988

Establishment South African officials have increasingly become a rare sight at major sporting events around the world.

In Seoul, South Korea, to attend the summer Olympic Games, I arrived at an official IOC hotel last Friday and was surprised to see Denis McIldowie, a long-standing, senior official of the unrecognised establishment Olympic body in South Africa.

He was being hosted by Reg Alexander, an IOC member from Kenya who was constantly at odds with his own government and still seemed sympathetic to white South Africa.

Several African IOC members strongly objected to McIldowie's presence, and personally complained to the IOC President. Today, we hear McIldowie has been told to leave the country.

I am sure other South Africans are present at the Games, but they are being discreet and attracting no attention.

Friday October 28th, 1988
The IOC has announced the creation of an Apartheid and Olympism Commission. I don't like the name, and have said so. Apartheid and Olympism are opposite concepts, and do not go together. It should have been the Olympism Against Apartheid Commission.

In any event, I have been asked to serve as an adviser to the Commission, and have agreed to do so. It is intended that we will meet every year, at the same time and place as the IOC session, and our task is to closely monitor the developing situation in South Africa and also engage various stakeholders inside and outside of the country to advance the end of apartheid in sport.

Judge Kéba Mbaye, of Senegal, a Vice President of the IOC and former Vice President of the International Court of Justice, has been appointed as Chairman of the Commission. He is an able man, and I am confident we will make rapid progress.

There is still much work to be done.

Saturday February 11th, 1989
Harry Gwala came to have dinner at our flat in Hampstead last night. We spoke for hours about the old days and ongoing changes in South Africa. It was a truly wonderful evening.

A teacher and politician from Pietermaritzburg, inland from Durban, he has earned the nickname Munt'omdala, or 'Lion of the Midlands', for his heroic contribution to the struggle.

His various involvements in political and trade union activities earned him two spells of imprisonment on Robben Island, from 1964 until 1972 and then again from 1977 until 1988. However, motor neuron disease robbed him of the use of his arms and this led to his release from prison in November 1988.

Disability, we saw for ourselves, had not defeated him.

Helga and I had suggested we would meet Harry at his hotel, but he insisted he would visit us at our home, even though it meant he would have to struggle up four flights of stairs.

"I told Sam I would meet him in his flat," he said, as he made steady progress, "and that's what I am going to do."

I cooked a meal, and listened to the stories of how Harry had taught history to his fellow prisoners on Robben Island, using The Bible, the only book provided by warders, as his text.

"So, Harry," I asked. "Will we see the end of apartheid?"

"It won't be long now," he replied, softly but with conviction. "I don't believe the day of liberation is very far away."

WATERSHED

Ian Hobbs, a journalist and a friend of mine in London, phoned during the first week of September 1989, and said he believed Ali Bacher was recruiting a rebel English squad to tour South Africa. The news didn't surprise me. After all, the South African Cricket Union (SACU) had been launching regular raids on international cricket for almost a decade.

Their prospectus was simple: suspend your conscience, ignore your morals, play in South Africa and take our money. A discredited sequence of Englishmen, Sri Lankans, West Indians and Australians had signed on the dotted line and defied the boycott.

SACU tried to justify this policy of spending millions of rands on rebel tours by citing their obligation to keep cricket alive in hard times. While they kept their business afloat, many millions of people continued to suffer. In effect, their selfish and shortsighted actions succeeded only in giving legitimacy to apartheid.

Ian said the English players were being contracted to make tours to South Africa in successive seasons, with the first tour due to start in January 1990. He had heard rumours that Mike Gatting, the former England captain, would agree to lead the team.

It was interesting news.

At any given time during the previous 17 years, I would have immediately relayed this kind of information to my colleagues at SACOS, the umbrella body for the nonracial sports movement with which I had been involved all those years ago.

Times had changed.

Instead, I telephoned Krish Naidoo, a leading member of the sports wing of the Mass Democratic Movement, an organisation that essentially represented the ANC inside South Africa, and told him to be prepared for a rebel English cricket tour.

Now, I am determined that this book, these reflections, should not become bogged down in the minutiae of political manoeuvring that inevitably characterise any period of transition.

For each meeting, there tends to be as many different versions of what happened as there were people in the room. Every person has his or her own sincerely held perspective on what happened, why it happened and who should get the credit.

Everyone is entitled to their own 'truth'.

For my part, I would like to set down the events that led to my estrangement from close friends at SACOS, the developments that meant, on that day in September 1989, I called not them but Krish Naidoo with news of the English cricket tour.

The bare facts are these.

Towards the end of the 1980s, the ANC leadership decided to revise its overall strategy and began to engage various white South Africans in discussions about the country's future.

I sat and listened to Oliver Tambo, the ANC leader, when he delivered the Canon Collins Memorial Lecture in London on May 28th, 1987, and heard him openly discuss engagement.

He spoke of a People's Culture fast emerging in South Africa, an alternative democratic power embracing politics, trade unionism, education, sport, religion and many other fields.

And he continued: "Indeed, the moment is upon us when we shall deal with the structures our people have created and are creating through struggle and sacrifice as the representatives of the masses. Not only should these not be boycotted, but more, they should be supported, encouraged and treated as the democratic counterparts within South Africa of similar institutions and organisations internationally. This means that the ANC, the broad democratic movement in all its forms within South Africa and the international solidarity movement must act together."

I listened, and understood. If the ANC believed it was time to engage on a broader political and social level, then I believed it was important that the sports struggle should follow suit, and ensure the entire movement advanced at the same pace.

The SANROC Executive agreed I should start making regular, almost monthly, visits to the ANC headquarters in Lusaka, where I would meet Barbara Masekela, who handled the ANC arts, culture and sports portfolio, and various other officials.

In fact, on one such visit, I had scarcely walked into my room at the Intercontinental Hotel in Lusaka, when the telephone started to ring. It was Steve Tshwete, another ANC leader, asking if I could immediately go to see him in another room.

Unbeknown to me, Steve had been meeting with a group of progressive whites from the Eastern Cape, and one of them happened to mention he would like to meet me.

Steve knew I was due to arrive in town that very evening, and replied casually: "Well, I can arrange that right away."

The white South Africans could hardly believe their eyes when I appeared at the door barely five minutes later.

Senior ANC leaders continued to attend clandestine meetings with eminent white South Africans, from enlightened politicians to Afrikaner intellectuals, in diverse venues worldwide, from New York hotels to African capitals to English country estates.

They met Frederik van Zyl Slabbert, the former leader of the official opposition, and others in Dakar; they met Louis Luyt, a prominent businessman, and others in Frankfurt.

These may have been talks about talks (and the South African government publicly feigned hostility to appease its powerful right wing constituency), but after three decades of violent hostility, the start of dialogue between white South Africa and the recognised black liberation movement was highly significant.

In September 1988, Essop Pahad, a leading ANC official, tracked me down to a hotel in Seoul, South Korea, where I was attending the Olympic Games, and informed me of a plan to meet Dr Danie Craven, President of the South African Rugby Board, and other white sports leaders in Harare.

"That's fine," I replied, "but we must be sensitive and ensure the non-racial sports movement in South Africa feels involved and is always kept fully informed of the process."

I said it would be embarrassing if Craven flew home after the meeting and made public statements that left the nonracial South African Rugby Union (SARU) feeling undermined or, worse, looking stupid because they didn't know a meeting had taken place.

Essop agreed and immediately accepted my suggestion that a SARU delegation, led by its President, Ebrahim Patel, should travel to meet ANC officials in Lusaka as soon as possible.

I called Gabu Tugwana in Johannesburg, a smart journalist at the *New Nation* newspaper who was also our SANROC representative in South Africa, and asked him to contact SARU and make all the necessary arrangements.

The meeting took place soon afterwards, and was considered to have been a complete success by both sides.

Unfortunately, SACOS was unhappy. In their view, facilitating a meeting between the ANC in exile and one of their member bodies amounted to an act of treachery.

While the ANC had started to talk, the SACOS leadership had remained adamant there should be no contact with the white sports establishment until apartheid had been erased.

I was publicly branded a 'traitor' to the cause for which I had dedicated most of my life and was effectively excommunicated from the organisation. Even today, I sense a degree of enmity towards me among several former members of SACOS.

This fundamental difference of opinion was exacerbated when Dennis Brutus, my mentor in the early days, declared from America that he shared the SACOS view. So, they turned their backs on me, and looked towards him as their external representative.

Polarisation ensued. In certain areas of the nonracial sports movement, you became either a 'Brutus man' or a 'Ramsamy man', and the wounds cut deep on all sides.

On reflection, I still see no fault in having adjusted my position to suit changing circumstances within the struggle. I made the right decision at the time, and it remains correct now.

Looking back over the past 15 years, I would argue the policy of engagement placed sport in the vanguard of reform, from where it has frequently sustained the transformation process by bringing South

Africans together under the rainbow flag.

On the other hand, SACOS leaders may claim the nonracial sports movement gave up too much too soon, agreeing unity at any cost with the result that, in many cases, transformation has been at best cosmetic and at worst a cynical deception.

I would claim substantial strides have been taken towards the provision of equal opportunities in sport for all South Africans, but they might say too many people in underprivileged areas are still denied basic facilities, equipment and coaching.

There is no absolute right, and no absolute wrong.

As I drifted apart from SACOS, I grew closer to members of the National Sports Congress (NSC), which was effectively the sports wing of the Mass Democratic Movement (MDM), an organisation that emerged after the UDF was prescribed and banned in 1985.

I was introduced to Bill Jardine, a strong, silver-haired, widely admired activist and to a bright, young lawyer named Krish Naidoo. "You should contact Naidoo," Gabu Tugwana told me, "but always call him at home in the evening, not at the office."

Gabu was always alert to the possibility of telephones being bugged – when he visited me in London, he was only completely comfortable if we spoke in my car with the radio switched on – but I had long since been reconciled to the reality that South African officials were bugging the telephones of all our associates.

The contrast between SACOS and the NSC was clear. While the SACOS hierarchy seemed to have contracted to a band of extreme left-wing philosophers, the NSC was part of a broader community-based organisation, aligned to the ANC, which the vast majority of South Africans recognised as their legitimate leaders.

At first, ANC officials adopted a conciliatory attitude towards SACOS but efforts to find common ground proved futile and, sadly, the anti-apartheid sports movement divided.

In October 1989, as the schism deepened, I was asked at short notice to attend a crucial meeting in Lusaka, but could only arrange to fly from London to Zambia for a single day.

Arriving on a Saturday morning, I drove to the home of Thabo

Mbeki, Head of the ANC's Foreign Affairs desk, where I found Barbara Masekela and Krish Naidoo had already arrived. We were gathered to discuss the general situation in the sports struggle.

I briefly outlined my perspective and said that, while it was infinitely preferable for SACOS to be persuaded to join the process, I had decided to cut all ties with the organisation.

Thabo Mbeki listened carefully, and said: "I realise it's painful for you, Sam, but you've made the right decision. As far as we are concerned, you are the recognised external representative of the nonracial sports movement inside South Africa."

He then gave us lunch – through the years, whenever we met at the Mbeki home, we always left with full stomachs – and we proceeded to discuss the English rebel cricket tour.

Krish Naidoo proposed that an NSC delegation should travel to London to meet players and officials from the rebel squad. He knew it would be difficult to make them change their minds but added at least the NSC officials could warn them to expect protests.

He said such a trip would also provide an opportunity to meet key British journalists, not only to secure positive coverage and set the media agenda in favour of the NSC and the demonstrators, but also perhaps even to develop contacts with sympathetic journalists who would supply valuable intelligence as the tour ran its course.

I was so impressed by Krish's process and planning that, when the issue of funding was raised, I said SANROC would meet the costs of the NSC delegation's visit to London.

With that, I had to excuse myself from the meeting, and rush to catch the overnight flight to England because I had long-standing commitments the next morning in London.

I had spent not even a full day in Lusaka but, as I relaxed into my seat on the plane, I sensed those few hours had represented a crossroads in my life. I asked for a glass of beer, reflected on what had been agreed, and felt happy with my decision.

It was clear to me that the ANC/MDM/UDF axis was a strong, broad-based movement with the capacity to advance the liberation struggle, end apartheid and broker unity and equal opportunities in

South African sport. I would not be disappointed.

The NSC dispatched a delegation to London, and I made sure I was at Heathrow Airport to welcome the group that included Krish Mackerdhuj, President of the nonracial South African Cricket Board, Ngconde Balfour, an activist from Cape Town, and Mi Hlatwayo, from the MDM in Durban.

After taking them to their hotel to freshen up, I drove them to my flat in Hampstead, where we began planning

In the days that followed, the delegation met David Graveney, the manager of the English rebel squad and, while he seemed to be reasonably progressive, he was committed to tour. They also met British journalists, and found allies for their cause.

As the countdown to the cricket tour continued, I maintained close contact with Krish Naidoo, and was not at all surprised when he asked for financial assistance to fund his plans.

He explained how the printers had agreed to charge only their costs in producing anti-tour pamphlets, and he told me how buses would be needed to ferry demonstrators to the match venues and that the bus companies had reduced their rates.

"Of course, we'll help," I said immediately.

This was a young lawyer who was taking time away from his practice and his family, simply because he believed in the cause. As much as anybody, he and the organisation that he was working so hard to mobilise deserved our complete support.

I made some calls… to the Swedish Sports Confederation in Stockholm, the Danish Youth Sports Movement in Copenhagen and to the Norwegian Sports Confederation in Oslo. Each of these bodies received funding from their respective governments and, as soon as I explained what was required, each contributed.

Our next task was to transfer these funds to the NSC in Johannesburg, and a solution emerged when the late Agie Mangera agreed to serve as a conduit. This committed businessman travelled regularly between London and South Africa and, each time he flew, he took some cash to Krish Naidoo.

A week before the English rebel cricketers were due to arrive in

Johannesburg, Krish called me to say they had planned a protest to take place at the airport, but said he was concerned the group of mostly young demonstrators could get overexcited.

He explained the youngsters needed a leader, somebody who they respected and who had experience of such stand-offs with the police. He asked if I could contact Winnie Mandela, and he provided me with her telephone number.

I said I would make a call, and get straight back to him.

"Comrade Sam," Winnie replied, "I will be there."

On the sunny morning of Friday January 19th, 1990, she was there at Jan Smuts Airport, in the midst of the action, demanding people be allowed to get off their buses and protest.

Rattled and concerned, the police drove at the demonstrators with batons and unleashed dogs. Even before the cricketers had touched down in South Africa – their flight was delayed – the violent tone of their ill-timed tour had been established.

Moss Mashishi, a young and highly effective publicity officer for the NSC, had also been in the midst of the fray, and he fulfilled an important role by filing regular reports to Radio 702, informing public opinion and setting a benchmark for all media.

During the three weeks that followed, I received first-hand reports from Krish and others, and watched the remarkable scenes unfold on the TV news bulletins in Britain.

For the first time, mainstream white South African sport was forced to confront the reality of black protest. They may have seen anti-tour demonstrations on television reports from Britain in 1969 and New Zealand in 1981, but they had never before witnessed the anger and taunts from just beyond the boundary.

In Kimberley, Pietermaritzburg and Bloemfontein, every day's play was overshadowed by the noisy presence of tens of thousands of disciplined demonstrators chanting and singing just outside the ground. The NSC was evidently doing a superb job.

As the days passed, I sensed the Gatting Tour, as it became known, was emerging as a watershed in the history of South African sport, a time when the past collided with the future.

Never again would the white sports establishment be able to dismiss their black counterparts. As their cocoon of arrogance and complacency was ripped apart, they were forced to accept the need to take blacks seriously, whether they liked it or not.

This bare-toothed confrontation created the atmosphere of recognition and respect in which sincere negotiations about a new sporting dispensation could begin. Effectively, the Gatting tour was the fiery furnace in which unity would be forged.

Those individuals who so effectively stoked the coals, notably Krish Naidoo, must be recognised in years to come.

By Friday, February 9th, it had become necessary to reduce the temperature. Three weeks of heated demonstrations had unfolded against a background of dramatic political events: on February 2nd, State President FW de Klerk had stood in Parliament and declared the unbanning of political organisations, including the ANC, and also his government's intention to free Nelson Mandela.

At lunchtime on the 9th, Thabo Mbeki phoned me in London.

"Sam, the protests have been going very well," he said.

"Yes," I replied, "exceptionally well."

"Let me tell you in confidence," he continued. "Madiba is going to be freed this weekend, and we don't want him released into an atmosphere of violence and disruption. We must contain the situation, and restore some kind of calm."

"I understand."

"Please tell your people to call off the troops," he concluded.

"I will do that," I replied, "but maybe you could also call Krish Naidoo today, just to explain the situation."

He agreed.

Two visiting officials from Sweden, two of our strongest supporters, Stig Hedlund and Walter Ronmark, happened to be seated in my office when I took this call, but neither of them had the slightest idea to whom I was talking or what we spoke about.

I apologised to them, and said I needed to make another call before we could continue our meeting. So, I phoned Krish, told him what was happening and to expect Mbeki's call.

Saturday, February 10th, was the third day of the unofficial Test at the Wanderers and Krish Naidoo had just got home after another day of demonstrations. A canister of tear gas had been let off in his eyes, and he needed medical treatment, but such cares evaporated when his telephone rang and Mbeki came on the line.

The message was clear and, that evening, Krish Naidoo and Bill Jardine sat down with Ali Bacher, and began to seek an agreement whereby the NSC would call off the protests and SACU would cancel, or curtail, the English tour. The meeting was eventually adjourned until the next morning.

Krish and I kept in regular telephone contact throughout, but little progress was made on the Sunday morning, and, around noon, the representatives decided to join millions of other people around the world, sitting in front of their televisions, watching the historic release of Nelson Mandela after 27 years in jail.

Sky News had asked me to join their broadcast of the events at the Victor Verster prison near Cape Town, so I was sitting in their Westminster studio, offering my perspective as the most celebrated political prisoner in the world finally walked free.

Bacher spent Monday at an emergency meeting of the SACU Board, Naidoo consulted extensively among his principals, and the pair agreed to meet again at 7.30 in the evening.

Krish told me that afternoon he felt a reasonable compromise would be for the English team to play three more matches, and for the scheduled second tour to be cancelled. I agreed.

During the course of the next eight hours, deep into the night, he must have called me at home every 45 minutes. I didn't mind at all because these were momentous times but, every time my wife Helga managed to fall asleep, the telephone rang again.

Eventually, after midnight in London, Krish called to say they had reached agreement: the English team would play four one-day matches against the South African team, and then go home, and the following year's second tour would be cancelled.

"The only problem," he continued, "is that we can't play any of those matches in Cape Town or the Eastern Cape because the protesters might get out of control, so we have to stage them in Centurion, Durban, Bloemfontein and Johannesburg."

"OK."

"But Krish Mackerdhuj absolutely refuses to allow any match on this tour to be played in Durban, his home town."

I said I would call the SACB President, and get back to Naidoo as soon as possible. It was now the early hours of the morning, but I managed to raise Krish Mackerdhuj and, when I had explained the overall situation, he reluctantly agreed to the deal.

Hardly pausing for breath, I phoned Krish Naidoo and told him everything was fine. "It's time for champagne," I told the young lawyer. "You and your people have done a fantastic job."

I look back on these dramatic events now, and believe they may well have been the single moment when victory was secured in our long, difficult struggle against apartheid in sport.

Of course, the Gatting tour happened to coincide with Nelson Mandela's release, and the effects of one should not be confused with the wider, greater ramifications of the other.

Yet, in sport, nothing was ever the same again.

The nonracial sports movement instantly gained confidence and never looked back. The process accelerated towards genuine administrative unification at every level, the launch of development programmes and full international readmission.

Across the barbed-wire barricades around the cricket ground in Kimberley, where black protesters and white fans traded insults and spat at each other, South African sport was speeding towards a precipice of self-destruction and catastrophe.

Somehow, mercifully, it applied the brakes, turned round and began to move away towards unity and reconciliation.

The main players in this drama also moved on: Ali Bacher was transformed from the mastermind of rebel cricket tours into one of the most visionary leaders in South African sport; Krish Naidoo soon left South Africa to study military affairs at Aberdeen, in Scotland, before returning home to resume his legal career.

As for me, the fast-developing situation presented me with a simple choice: do I stay in London, having done my job and helped to secure change, or do I go home, and help implement change?

In February 1990, I was undecided.

GOING HOME

The journalist asked whether I was looking forward to going home to South Africa and, all of a sudden, the question seemed more complicated than I ever imagined it would be. It was the mid-1980s, and I wasn't sure. The end of apartheid still seemed much more than a lifetime away.

"Well," I replied, dragging my words, "I have always thought that, after liberation, it would be nice to retire to a small house on the Durban beachfront and live quietly."

Chris Whitfield, who went on to be Editor of the *Cape Times*, noted my words, but they didn't carry much conviction. Would I live to see the day of liberation? Nobody could be sure.

Through the late 1980s, as the reform process gathered pace, the prospect of going home came into a sharper process but, even then, I seriously doubted whether I would be able to return and play any kind of active role in South African sport.

In many ways, I felt tired. In my mind, the imminent end of our campaign opened the appealing prospect of going home, being reunited with my friends and family, and doing nothing more than getting up to see the sun rise out of the Indian ocean.

It would not be easy to leave London.

People had told me to avoid growing roots in exile and yet, in a period which represented two thirds of my adult life, it had been impossible not to develop a circle of friends and a lifestyle. Did we now want to leave all that and start all over again?

There is a romanticised view of exiles as men and women who are forced to leave their homeland and settle abroad, where they gaze dreamily out of the window until the day dawns when they can return home in triumph and fulfil their destiny. But, this was not the reality for many of those South Africans who had to flee their country during the 1960s and 1970s.

111

There are many who settled abroad, built careers abroad, married abroad and raised children abroad. Then, when the day arrived for them to return to South Africa, it suddenly felt as if they would not be so much going home as leaving home.

Imperceptibly, year-by-year, they had become Norwegian or British or Swedish or Danish or Canadian or Australian. Their spouses often came from their adopted country and, to their children, South Africa was a strange place their father sometimes spoke about, far removed from what they knew and trusted as their home.

For every one South African exile who did return home and settled happily, there is one who remains abroad, making the best of it, reconciled to life in limbo, estranged from the land of his birth and yet never truly accepted by his adopted nation, sentenced by circumstance to a permanent, unending exile.

My situation was less severe. Unencumbered by children and blessed with a supportive wife always prepared to embrace a new challenge, I never stopped wanting to return home.

The question was when.

During one of my regular visits to ANC officials in Lusaka, one evening over drinks, I happened to mention some of these issues to Barbara Masekela and Steve Tshwete.

"You must go back now and get involved," Barbara said.

"I'm not sure," I mumbled.

"No question," said Steve, smiling and, typically, becoming almost lyrical. "There is a tough road ahead for South African sport, with many rocks, and we want you in the driving seat.

"It won't be easy. We may have to turn left at times; we may have to turn right at times. Sometimes, we may even have to go in reverse, but we certainly need you at the wheel."

"Well, let's see how things go," I said.

"I'm serious," he repeated.

"OK."

Through the weeks and months that followed the conclusion of the Gatting tour, I remained at the SANROC office in London and, wherever and whenever possible, assisted in the process of establishing the National

Sports Congress as the dominant macro-sports body in South Africa.

We provided funds: in 1989, we had paid the bus and hotel costs for delegates attending a NSC workshop at Wits University, and we also contributed to the costs of the formal launch of the organisation in 1990.

We recommended a name change: the establishment Olympic Committee was proclaiming itself worldwide as the only specific Olympic body in South Africa, so the NSC quickly became known as the NOSC, the National Olympic and Sports Congress.

We gave input to the Constitution: Krish Naidoo took on the task of writing this document and, with simplicity and clarity, placed the NOSC on three pillars – unity, development and participation, in that order. First, we would seek unity, then development, and only then participation in international competition.

It was a clever strategy because it plainly set the agenda for the establishment white sports administrators who focussed on an end to isolation: that could only happen when unity was secured and development programmes had been launched.

There were no short cuts. The only route back to world sport was through the new nonracial sports structures, and the NOSC had shrewdly positioned itself at the gateway.

The organisation was officially launched in June 1990, at a function in Cape Town, courtesy of a R50 000 cheque anonymously granted by the PG Glass organisation.

On the same day, the three major nonracial federations, in rugby, cricket and football, broke away from SACOS and affiliated to the new NOSC.

In due course, Mluleki George, an activist who had broken his neck playing rugby and been repeatedly tortured by the South African Security Police before eventually being sent to prison on Robben Island for three years, was elected as President, and Mthobi Tyamzashe became Secretary-General.

I watched from afar, tried to assist if required, and was highly impressed by the rate of progress.

In less than a year, a group of individuals, assembled as the sports wing of an underground political movement, albeit one that happened to be associated with the massively influential ANC, had effectively taken control of sport in South Africa.

The selfless dedication to the cause, which made such swift and spectacular progress possible, was evident in many, and vividly personified in the example of Mthobi Tyamzashe.

He was working for Johnson and Johnson in East London when he became involved in the nonracial sports movement, but, as the weeks passed, he began to spend more and more time on his work for the NSC, handling faxes and making telephone calls.

If something needed to be done, he just did it. However, his employers expressed concern that he was not giving enough time to his actual job, and they terminated his employment.

The NSC Executive responded by appointing Mthobi to a paid position, as the full-time Secretary-General, and, although his salary was meagre in the early days, he was later promoted to be Director- General in the Ministry of Sport and Recreation.

Meanwhile in London, a measure of intensity seemed to be draining away from our campaign. The 1990 Commonwealth Games took place successfully in Christchurch, New Zealand with scarcely a mention of South Africa. A Labour government had transformed New Zealand from collaborators with apartheid sport into steadfast opponents, and African nations happily competed.

Juan Antonio Samaranch, the IOC President, had taken note of these developments, and, at a meeting of the IOC Olympism and Apartheid Commission in Kuwait, he suggested an African solution should be found to this African problem, and charged the Association of National Olympic Committees of Africa (ANOCA) to guide the IOC on if and when South Africa should be readmitted.

The ANOCA President, Jean-Claude Ganga, then asked me to visit South Africa as a one-man commission and report back to him, ANOCA and the IOC Commission on what I found.

"Talk to as many people as you can," said my close friend through two decades of struggle against apartheid sport.

So, on August 11th, 1990, I walked into the Arrivals Area at Johannesburg Airport, almost 18 years and five months after I had slipped into exile through the selfsame building, and was welcomed as a long-lost friend by Johan du Plessis, President of the white South African National Olympic Committee.

My visit had been widely previewed in the media but, if I had been slightly apprehensive about the nature of my reception, those fears did not last long. At this stage, the white sports fraternity saw me as the person who held the key to readmission, and, to secure that Holy Grail, they would do almost anything, even welcome an enemy who had campaigned for their isolation.

I may have been relieved, but I was not fooled.

When Du Plessis was quoted in a newspaper eulogising me as 'a hero who had given South Africans a new vision of the road ahead', I remembered a line somewhere in Shakespeare about lions making leopards tame, but not changing their spots.

Of course, I was prepared to reconcile, unify and move on, but not to roll over and have my tummy tickled.

In South Africa, I met Nelson Mandela in Johannesburg where he stressed his commitment to negotiation and reconciliation, and was taken by Ronnie Pillay, now a judge, to visit Govan Mbeki in the township of New Brighton, near Port Elizabeth.

I was inspired by both meetings, and suddenly found myself feeling wonderfully positive about the prospect of returning home and helping such extraordinary men build a new South Africa.

Kader Asmal, an Executive member of SANROC, joined me on my journey from Durban, and had travelled with me to meet Mbeki in New Brighton. As we hurtled around the country, every minute of every day seemed so interesting and captivating.

We had both lived so far away for so long that, in many ways, we felt as if we were visiting a brand-new country.

In Cape Town, I met officials of SACOS, an organisation that had meant so much to me ever since its conception, but from which I was now sadly estranged. I greeted Joe Ebrahim, the President, and we both tried to be constructive, but relations were strained.

To my amazement, SACOS had arranged for their supporters to stage a protest against me, outside the venue of our meeting.

Of course, there was a certain irony in the fact that somebody who had organised anti-apartheid demonstrations around the world should now be the target of protest by his former colleagues, but I was deeply disappointed by the experience.

Did I want to get involved in sport when I returned home and find this type of antagonism? Had I become such a divisive element that my presence would be counter-productive?

I didn't know the answers, but there was no time to reflect as Kader and I followed our itinerary, meeting officials of sports federations from both the establishment and the nonracial movement.

Twenty-six meetings in the space of eight days left me with the impression that, with few exceptions, the political and sporting leadership on both sides subscribed to the NOSC mantra of unity, then development, then participation.

This seemed to be a sound base for progress, and that was the gist of my report to Jean-Claude Ganga, when I met with him in Brazzaville, Congo, after leaving Johannesburg.

Events were beginning to assume their own momentum. Just three weeks later, attending the fourth International Conference Against Apartheid in Stockholm, Jean-Claude and I reported back to Samaranch and discussed the next step.

"So, you say there are four umbrella sporting bodies in South Africa plus SANROC," the IOC President asked. "Correct?"

I nodded, almost apologetically.

"Well, we must get them all together," he said.

We agreed such a meeting should take place outside South Africa. Jean-Claude proposed Harare as the most accessible venue, and arrangements were quickly made for representatives of the five organisations – the establishment SANOC, COSAS, a largely white group, the NOSC, SACOS and SANROC – to assemble in the Zimbabwean capital on November 3rd and 4th, 1990.

The IOC allocated some funds to meet costs, and I took care to ensure this money was discreetly channelled to buy the air tickets and pay the hotel bills of those delegates from the nonracial sports movement who could least afford them. Tommy Sithole, President of the Zimbabwe

National Olympic Committee, helped with the arrangements.

So, we arrived from opposite points on the political compass. Long-standing enemies looked each other in the eye, shook hands, sat down and began to identify common goals. The scale of what happened in Harare 1990 should not be overlooked.

In practical terms, the meeting agreed to form a new body to be called the Co-ordinating Committee for Sport in South Africa (CCSSA). This would be comprised of two representatives from each of the five organisations, and would plot the way forward.

For the best part of a year, I had been trying to make up my mind precisely when to return home, but evolving events had made the decision for me. In line to play a leading role in South Africa's new national Olympic body, D-Day had arrived.

Helga and I hosted a small New Year's party to say goodbye and thank you to our close friends in London, especially those from SANROC and the wider Anti-Apartheid Movement.

We also arranged to rent out the flat in Hampstead, packed up our belongings into a few boxes and prepared to leave the city that had given us refuge and inspiration for so long,

We arrived in Johannesburg on January 9th, 1991, excited by the challenge that lay ahead but under no illusion that our new lives in South Africa would always be relaxed.

All thoughts of retiring by the beachfront in Durban had evaporated like the morning haze that often hangs on the horizon, and we suspected tough times lay ahead.

We were not wrong.

The CCSSA met in earnest, in Johannesburg on January 12th, 1991, and I was elected as Chairman of the committee.

Maybe people believed that, having been a London-based outsider for so long, I was well placed to arrive back in town and preside over the rival local bodies. Perhaps, my strong association with the IOC also weighed significantly in my favour.

Certainly, I had not campaigned or lobbied for any leadership role. It had been offered to me and I had accepted, and, as I did so, I recalled how, many months before in the cool of a Lusaka evening, Steve Tshwete had said he wanted me in the driving seat. And, by January 1991, that is where I seemed to be sitting... back home, ready to start a new phase of my life.

RUSHING TO BARCELONA

Almost 30 years after we first met at the Olympic Games in Munich, Jean-Claude Ganga was still watching my back. "Sam," he said softly. "I smell something." It did not surprise either my friend from the Congo or me that certain people would be working hard to prevent me from becoming the leader of South Africa's new Olympic body.

Our information suggested certain officials of the National Party government, and its paid representatives at the South African embassy in Switzerland, were trying to persuade IOC leaders that I was simply not the right man to be Chairman.

Their argument was purely racial: they argued I would not be an acceptable Chairman for either the blacks or the whites because I was of Indian origin, and represented a small minority.

Their motivation was purely personal: they could not bear the idea that the individual who had campaigned for the sports boycott should return and take a prominent leadership role.

It was to be expected that remnants of the departing regime should have harboured a grudge against me, but I was surprised they had been able to poison certain IOC officials, notably Francois Carrard, the Director-General, against me.

"I smell something," said Jean-Claude Ganga. "Something is not right. People are working against you, Sam."

Several discreet telephone calls to old friends revealed a plan whereby one or two members of the IOC Commission on Olympism and Apartheid were intending to visit South Africa in March, execute an ambush and install someone else as Chairman.

I had thought these people were my friends, as I had worked as a Special Adviser to their Commission, and enjoyed their company.

"If they have a problem with me, why don't they just come out and say so," I asked Jean-Claude. "I don't understand why they have had to be so devious and clandestine."

"Don't worry about that," he replied firmly. "We can resolve this issue. We, as ANOCA, will call a meeting of the Co-ordinating Committee as soon as possible, and then create an interim Olympic Committee with you as Chairman. When the IOC arrives in April, it will be too late for them to change anything."

So, it was done.

ANOCA met the Co-ordinating Committee for Sport in South Africa (CCSSA) on March 9th, 1991, in Gaborone, at the generous invitation of Ismail Bhamjee, President of the Botswana NOC. We formally created INOCSA, the Interim National Olympic Committee of South Africa, and I was installed as Chairman.

Three days later, Jean-Claude Ganga phoned to say he had been called by Judge Keba M'baye, Chairman of the IOC Olympism and Apartheid Commission, and admonished for his role in getting INOCSA off the ground sooner than expected.

"I think we took the wind out of their sails," he said.

The process rumbled on, running on a daily diet of rumours, private deals, covert tactics and ultimatums.

SACOS withdrew soon after the meeting in Gaborone, saying the process was moving too quickly. They claimed the need for real transformation was being overlooked in a crazed dash for unity to enable readmission and bank the financial bonanza.

In a pure sporting context, I understood precisely what they were saying and essentially agreed with them.

However, while they considered sport alone, I believed it was necessary to appreciate the broader picture. Into 1991, sport began to play an important, trail-blazing role within the wider political and social transformation, and it was our responsibility as sports leaders to accelerate our talks and keep moving forward.

We had to get South Africans playing sport together as soon as possible, and to bring the dream of one united country to life on the sports fields, both at home and abroad.

At times, I did feel as if we were moving too fast and, like any speeding

Two distinguished South Africans join me in celebrating my election as a member of the International Olympic Committee in July 1995: in the middle, Steve Tshwete, the Minister of Sport and Recreation, who played a key role in the unity process and, right, Kader Asmal, who returned from exile in Ireland to serve in the Cabinet.

Mthobi Tyamzashe, on my right, played a major role in the transition, first as Secretary-General of the National Sports Congress (NSC) and then as Director-General in the Department of Sport and Recreation.

Alan Knott-Craig, the Chief Executive Officer of Vodacom, has been a fervent and loyal supporter of the Olympic movement in South Africa and is a close personal friend.

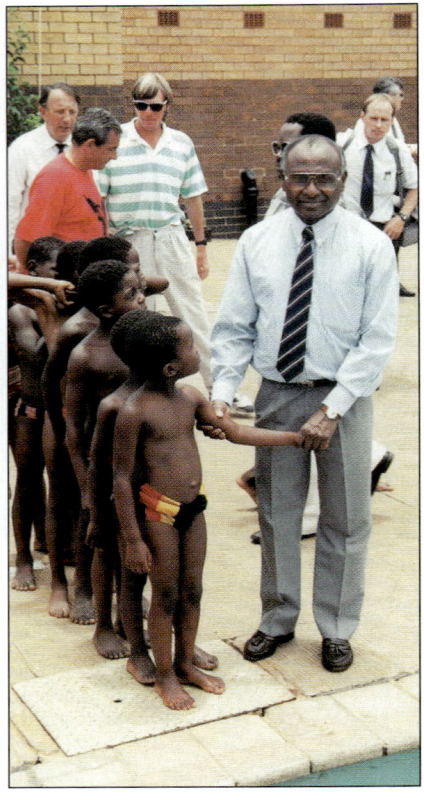

Jean-Claude Ganga, in the middle above, played a critical role in creating the new NOCSA. Here he is visiting the home of Oliver and Adelaide Tambo, with Khaya Ngqula, an important member of the NOCSA team, standing to the right. Soon, we were able to initiate development programmes nationwide, right.

South Africa was welcomed back into the fold at the 1992 Olympic Games in Barcelona, and I was privileged to march at the head of the team at the Opening Ceremony.

As President and ever since, Nelson Mandela has been an enthusiastic supporter of NOCSA, never more so than during Cape Town's bid to host the 2004 Olympic Games. The city finished third, behind Athens and Rome.

The legendary three-time Olympic heavyweight boxing champion Teofilo Stevenson, of Cuba, was one of several sporting celebrities who visited South Africa to endorse NOCSA's formation and progress.

I was honoured to serve on the organising committee for the inauguration of President Mandela in 1994, and I took responsibility for organising the football match between South Africa and Zambia at Ellis Park on the afternoon following the inauguration. The new President arrived at half-time, and was greeted by deafening acclamation.

Thomas Bach, an IOC member from Germany, middle, and Matthias Kleinert, Senior Vice-President of DaimlerChrysler, are well respected around the world and have been enthusiastic supporters of NOCSA.

The 1996 Olympic Games in Atlanta did not pass without problems, but there was no doubting the personal charm exuded by President Bill Clinton at this reception, with IOC President Juan Antonio Samaranch at his side.

Penny Heyns's gold medal performance in Atlanta provided a catalyst for Olympic enthusiasm in South Africa, and this genuinely world-class swimmer has emerged as a wonderfully positive role model.

Mustapha Larfaoui, right, was a strong ally in the fight against apartheid, and, as the current president of FINA, the world governing body of swimming, remains a close and valued colleague and friend.

Josiah Thugwane, middle, and Hezekiel Sepeng, right, flew home from Atlanta to a hero's reception. Thugwane's unforgettable gold medal in the marathon and Sepeng's silver medal in the 800 metres opened the minds of millions to Olympic achievement.

President Thabo Mbeki has been a strong supporter of NOCSA and is photographed here with, in the back row, from the left, Moss Mashishi, a key member of NOCSA, and the reverend Frank Chikane. The late Steve Tshwete is seated on the right. This photograph was taken by my wife, Helga.

Nelson Mandela's immense contribution to South Africa's progress in recent years cannot be overstated, and he remains a national inspiration to all. Here, I am visiting his house in Johannesburg with celebrated South African film maker, Anant Singh.

Zanele Mbeki, above left, South Africa's First Lady and a fervent supporter of NOCSA, travelled with the South African team to the 2000 Olympic Games in Sydney, and offered words of encouragement to our athletes. Terence Parkin, right, won a silver medal in the pool in what was a generally underrated performance by the South African team.

As is becoming usual, the South African team certainly did not lack enthusiasm when they marched in the Opening Ceremony at the Olympic Games in Sydney.

Jacques Rogge, above middle, has made a swift and positive impression since his election as IOC President in 2001. He was Guest of Honour at a NOCSA banquet in Johannesburg in 1998. George Bizos, the highly respected human rights lawyer, stands on the right.

Five smiles on the road to the 2004 Olympic Games in Athens are provided by, from left to right, IOC President Jacques Rogge, Gianna Angelopoulos, driving force behind the Greek Organising Committee, and my fellow IOC members, Toni Khouri and Alex Gilady.

vehicle, we risked losing control and a collision, but we were driven by an irrepressible momentum for sport to lead the national process, to be the catalyst for change and unity.

Bolstered by the constant support and encouragement, both in private and in public, of Nelson Mandela, Thabo Mbeki and Barbara Masekela, we could not fail.

So, INOCSA took shape as an eight-man committee plus me as Chairman. Sylvester Stein and Khaya Ngqula took their places as representatives of SANROC, and we diligently prepared ourselves to apply for formal recognition from the IOC. The IOC Commission on Olympism and Apartheid delegation arrived in Johannesburg, took a look around, had to deal with me as Chairman of the local committee whether they liked it or not, and bestowed on INOCSA a kind of conditional blessing.

At the end of the visit, their statement read: "Recognition will be granted to INOCSA on condition that apartheid be abolished and that INOCSA be formed into a democratically elected body which complies in structure and aims with the Olympic Charter, having as members unified, non-racial codes of Olympic sports."

Back in January, I had speculated that South Africa might be prepared to send a team to the 1996 Olympic Games in Atlanta, and been criticised for being premature. Only three months later, events had moved so fast that IOC officials were saying there was no good reason why South African athletes should not compete at the 1992 Olympic Games in Barcelona.

Foreign Prime Ministers, such as Bob Hawke, of Australia, and John Major, of Britain, began speculating that a lifting of the sports boycott would serve to encourage and reward the white community along the road to meaningful political reform.

This was dangerous talk. By all means, sport could be used to assist wider reform, but it should not be abused with its needs being swept away by the flood of political expediency. At the next meeting of INOCSA, I attempted to apply the brakes.

"We must not forget where we started," I told my colleagues. "Unity, development, participation: in that order. Now, that we have achieved unity, we must launch efficient development programmes to create equal opportunities, and we must do that before we return to international sport."

Sensing the representatives of COSAS and SANOC had started to shuffle in their seats, I continued: "If we are not ready to send a team to the Olympic Games in Barcelona next year, then we must simply accept it, be patient and stay at home."

As I looked at the faces around me, I saw some members of the Committee whom I trusted, some I didn't know well and some who, I felt certain, were already plotting against me. I had no time to worry about conspiracies. We needed to unite, and had to keep moving.

Helga and I had settled comfortably in Johannesburg. At first, we were based at the Carlton Hotel, but before long we moved into a small, functional flat in Rosebank. Oddly enough, the apartment had just been vacated by the great English footballer, Sir Stanley Matthews, who spent some years in South Africa. We are still happily living there today.

Initially, I worked from the SANOC offices, but the mood was uneasy and, after a while, I gratefully accepted Ali Bacher's offer of space in the United Cricket Board offices at the Wanderers. This was a charitable gesture, because they didn't actually have space and, when I was around, Ali usually worked from home. Such kindness is not easily forgotten.

The IOC convention was that, to be allowed to send a team to the Olympic Games, a National Olympic Committee must have been recognised by the IOC for at least one calendar year. So, after a preliminary visit to IOC headquarters in May, I led our delegation back to Lausanne for the occasion when INOCSA was to be formally recognised by the IOC.

Samaranch called me forward and gave me a letter of recognition and, in that act, on July 9th, 1991, INOCSA was transformed into NOCSA, the National Olympic Committee of South Africa.

As I walked back to my seat, I somehow caught Jean-Claude Ganga's eye. He was beaming. "It is for this we have been fighting these past 23 years," he said. I swallowed hard.

My plan was to join the rest of the delegation and fly back to Johannesburg that same evening, but, a few days earlier, I had been called by Colin Cowdrey, President of the International Cricket Council, and asked to fly home via London.

"I think we're going to readmit South Africa to the ICC," the Englishman told me, "and I would like you to be present."

Reissuing my ticket, and seeing no extra cost was involved in changing the route, I booked a flight to London.

South African cricket had hurtled to unity and readmission as fast as we had rushed to the IOC, although in fairness a sincere and established development programme eased their path. I had tried to assist at various stages, once kick-starting unity talks by pretending a donation of R10 000 to the nonracial South African Cricket Board had come from SANROC when, in truth, it had been raised by the South African Cricket Union.

Later, unreported, I endorsed the UCB's application in private discussions with High Commissioners from the Caribbean, whom I had got to know in London, and I also kept contact with Colin Cowdrey, a great listener, a fine diplomat and a gentleman.

Steve Tshwete, the ANC spokesman on Sport, played a huge role in helping Ali Bacher to persuade doubting officials in Asia and the West Indies that South African cricket was worthy of a return to the international arena, and it was during this frenetic period that I referred to Steve as 'Mr Fix-it".

There had once been a television programme in Britain called *Jim'll Fix It*, where viewers sent their dreams to a disc jockey called Jimmy Saville and he made some of them come true.

When South Africa needed unity in sport, it was invariably Steve who arrived to chair the key meeting and fix the divisions. He became Mr Fix-it to everyone, and the name stuck.

So, on the evening of July 10th, 1991, safely arrived in London from Lausanne, I walked into the Long Room at Lord's and attended a banquet to celebrate South Africa's readmission.

As I looked at the portraits of great cricketers on the walls, of Don Bradman, Lord Harris and others, I considered how, for many years, I was probably not the most popular man within these famous walls.

Happily, times had changed and I enjoyed the occasion.

The following evening, Colin Cowdrey took the South African cricket delegation, and me, for drinks with a passionate cricket fan, living at No 10 Downing Street. British Prime Minister John Major appeared both interested and progressive.

Meanwhile at NOCSA, all anyone wanted to know was if we would send a team to the Olympics in Barcelona.

My instinctive response was that we were just not ready, but I recognised it would be hard to resist both the sense of anticipation among the public and the ANC's enthusiasm for international sport as a vehicle for morale-building transformation.

IOC President Juan Antonio Samaranch seemed eager as well. The return of this prodigal African son would unite the Olympic family before the Games were hosted in his home town.

The pressure started to build.

Primo Nebiolo, leader of the world athletics body, was alert to the commercial opportunity and asked for South African athletes to attend the 1991 IAAF World Championships in Tokyo. This approach was declined: it was, everyone agreed, too soon.

Eventually, after consulting the ANC, NOCSA took a decision to accept the IOC invitation to participate at the summer Olympic Games of 1992 in Barcelona.

In October the Commonwealth Heads of Government Meeting (CHOGM) in Harare approved the creation of the Commonwealth Committee on Co-operation Through Sport, which was designed to assist sport in developing countries. In that context, the meeting endorsed South Africa's readmission to international sport.

We had nine months to get ready; they would prove nine of the most unpleasant, difficult months of my life.

I wanted to reconcile and negotiate a middle way, to nurture a new and inclusive Olympic Committee, but, over and over again, I was opposed, confronted and vilified by representatives of the old South Africa who still regarded me as the enemy.

Perhaps life would have been tolerable if such opposition was confined to right wing newspapers like *The Citizen, Die Beeld, Die Burger* and *Rapport*, or even if it festered only in the National Party and other inherently conservative political parties.

In fact, what made everything particularly difficult was that such hostility existed within a few members of the NOCSA Executive Committee, itself. Like Iago, my colleagues would smile, and smile again.

At one Executive meeting, we discussed the issue of language. and it was proposed, for convenience sake, that NOCSA should conduct its business in English, and this was agreed unanimously.

Many South African companies adopted similar policies at this time, but their Chairmen were not lambasted in the following day's newspapers as an enemy of the Afrikaans language. That was my fate.

Since we had not informed our member federations or issued a media release, it was obvious that a member of the Executive had leaked and distorted the news to put me in a bad light. Under pressure, I found my greatest support from Mluleki George, then Vice-President of NOCSA and President of the NSC.

As the weeks passed, I became amazed by the number of white South Africans who appeared to believe that, after 44 years of apartheid, it was necessary only to release Mandela, repeal several laws and rehearse some platitudes for everything to be normalised and everyone to live happily ever after.

Such people seriously believed it would be appropriate for the celebrated new nonracial South African Olympic team to march into the stadium behind the old national flag, the orange, white and blue symbol that for so long represented apartheid.

They were also insensitive enough to expect that their black compatriots would instantly forget the past and enthusiastically adopt 'Die Stem', the old national anthem, as their own.

A line needed to be drawn.

I tabled some proposals, eagerly supported by Mluleki, and the NOCSA Executive agreed, again unanimously, that our team would march behind a neutral flag in Barcelona and would use the Olympic hymn, Beethoven's 'Ode to Joy', as our anthem if one of our athletes won a gold medal.

This was not unusual: another country in transition in 1992, the former Soviet Union, planned to call themselves the 'United Team' and to use the Olympic hymn as their anthem.

Was it going to be too much to expect that, in return for black endorsement of readmission and the dash to Barcelona, white South Africa at large would accept these interim symbols? Yes, it was.

Our decisions were taken at the same time as the National Party was holding its Transvaal Congress, and the delegates united in outrage against NOCSA in general, and me in particular.

State President De Klerk was critical. Louis Pienaar, Minister of National

Education, with responsibility for sport, said our decision was 'a slap in the face for all South Africans' and angrily threatened to retaliate by withholding funds from NOCSA.

Jaap Marais, leader of the extreme Herstigte Nasionale Party, the HNP, went further, accusing me of contravening the Constitution by treating the national flag with contempt. He instructed the South African Police to investigate criminal charges.

I resisted this onslaught, quietly telling myself NOCSA was making decisions that might have upset a vocal minority but which were fully supported and appreciated by the silent majority.

In the eye of a media storm, exactly when I needed support, several colleagues on the NOCSA Executive, all of whom had joined me in the unanimous decision, said nothing in public. They looked the other way and effectively hung me out to dry. Were they involved in this orchestrated campaign to discredit me? Or were these men just scared? I didn't know.

Every week brought a new headline. It was almost as though the old National Party warriors had reconciled themselves to the reality of power-sharing and the end of apartheid, but they were damned if they were going to stand by and let Sam Ramsamy, their old enemy, take a leading role in the new dispensation.

The depth of their animosity was startling. They hated me, but the intensity of their revulsion was matched by my plain resolve to survive, withstand the attacks and prevail.

Earlier in the year, they had tried to engulf me in a corruption scandal in local football because one of the football officials, Abdul Bhamjee, gave me a watch as a birthday present.

The connection was entirely spurious but, again, day after day, stories were fed to the same right-wing newspapers and the headlines raged, bombarding me with unsubstantiated claims in the desperate hope that some mud would stick.

All of a sudden, the watch was valued at R70 000, when it cannot have been worth a fraction of that amount. The allegations were spectacularly pumped up like a balloon, but they were popped by the needle of truth, and quickly disintegrated.

My policy throughout this unsettling period was to ignore the attacks and carry on working at NOCSA, laying foundations for our organisation and preparing the team for Barcelona, content in the knowledge that I had done nothing wrong.

In difficult times, I used to recall the advice once given to me by Richard Caborn, a close friend of ours in London who was then a prominent member of the Anti-Apartheid Movement and has since become an MP and Minister for Sport in Britain.

"Stay clear of sex and money," he often used to say, "and, whatever they do, they won't be able to touch you."

It's a sound adage. I lead a clean life because, over the years, I have learned something very simple and very true: the best form of defence against any accusation is innocence.

Our preparations to participate at the 1992 Olympic Games continued amid uncertainty as the general mood of the country rode the rollercoaster of political negotiations. One day, a breakthrough would prompt wild optimism; the next day, a setback would send everyone scurrying back to their racial trenches.

We managed to negotiate the peaks and troughs, but were almost derailed by the appalling events of June 17th, 1992, in the Western Transvaal region of Boipatong, when more than 40 people were massacred in what was called political violence.

However, it became widely suspected that the South African government was somehow involved.

In grief and outrage, ANC leaders decided to withdraw from the 'outreach programme', and that, after all, South Africa should not send a team to the Olympic Games. Even Archbishop Tutu asked for the international sports boycott to be imposed again.

Cyril Ramaphosa, then Secretary-General of the ANC, requested a meeting to convey this message to NOCSA, but I believed this was a moment when we needed to explain our dilemma.

I started by emphasising we shared their anger at what had happened and informed them that, as Interim Chairman of NOCSA, I had decided that I would travel to Boipatong and personally convey our condolences to the families of the victims.

"However, please bear this in mind," I continued, diplomatically. "We were not eager to participate in Barcelona, but we agreed because the ANC encouraged us to accept the invitation, saying it was in the broader interests of transformation.

"So, we gave our word to the IOC that we would send a team. Now, I must tell you that a decision to withdraw would be extremely difficult and would cause great embarrassment."

They listened and, after a discussion, it was agreed that South Africa would compete at the Games, but that our athletes would wear badges showing their support for peace. The IOC gave its official approval for the gesture, and the crisis passed.

Through the weeks preceding our departure for Spain, I had become increasingly concerned by the fact that the vast majority of elite athletes in our member federations, notably shooting, canoeing, sailing and many more, were white.

Since only a handful of black athletes – a few boxers, a few track athletes and Cheryl Roberts, in table tennis – had achieved Olympic qualifying standards, the complexion of our team was going to be overwhelmingly white.

Like everyone else, from the IOC to the ANC, we wanted the new South African team to reflect the demography of the new South Africa, but this was simply not going to be possible.

A meeting was arranged, where I explained the situation, and I remember how Steve Tshwete listened carefully, resting his head on his finger, as he used to do, deep in thought.

I asked: "How shall we handle this?"

"Sam," he replied, "we might not like it but, between you and me, we have no option but to accept it."

He was right. Nonetheless, NOCSA did convene a meeting of the federations, and conveyed our determination that meaningful development programmes should be introduced as soon as possible to ensure more representative teams in future.

I was still uncomfortable with the situation. Was this what we had fought for? Had we worked so hard to lead a team, which was 95 percent white, back into the Olympic movement?

Eventually, I suggested NOCSA should apply to the IOC for permission to bring to Barcelona an additional development team, comprised of 25 black athletes with potential who would march in the Opening Ceremony but not actually compete.

Yet again, Nelson Mandela demonstrated his support for our cause by agreeing to travel with me and Mluleki George to Lausanne to make what was a totally unprecedented request to the IOC President.

Samaranch was sympathetic to our unique situation, and gave his consent, even though, upon our arrival at the Games, it took me another two hectic days to convince officials of the Local Organising Committee that everything was in order and that our development squad should be allowed to take part in the Opening Ceremony.

So, somehow, somewhat breathlessly, we reached Barcelona, and conveyed a powerful image of reconciliation. The ostensibly equal mix of blacks and whites that marched into the Olympic stadium on a warm and emotional evening might not have been an accurate representation of what we were in 1992, but it was an honest expression of what we wanted to be.

Our flag was carried by Jan Tau, a black marathon runner, and, demonstrating our determination to build unity on a history of division, our team included an experienced 1 500m athlete by the name of Zola Budd.

She had left Britain and returned home in 1988, reasserted her South African citizenship and secured her place in the Olympic team on the strength of her performances.

In fact, soon after I arrived back in South Africa, I decided to attend an athletics meeting in Pretoria. As I approached the Pilditch stadium that evening, I immediately recognised the still slight and still young woman standing by the gates.

We greeted each other.

The past was buried, but it was odd to consider that, just four years after working so hard to keep her out of the Olympic Games in Seoul, I would be marching into the Olympic Stadium, at the head of a team that included Zola Budd.

Reconciliation was infectious. I also invited Rudolf Opperman, veteran leader of the establishment Olympic body in South Africa, to join us in Barcelona. He may have been my adversary in the past but, if Mandela could forgive, then so could we.

It was fitting that the ANC leader, who had done so much to get us there, should attend the Opening Ceremony, himself, and he seemed to enjoy the spectacle from the Stand of Honour.

On several occasions since, when he sees me and people are around, and, as usual, he is smiling, Madiba takes delight in telling everyone: "You should have seen Sam that night in Barcelona. He walked into the stadium as if he owned the place."

Over the 16 days that followed, considering the rushed nature of our preparations, it was remarkable that South Africa managed to win two medals at the Olympic Games of 1992.

Wayne Ferreira and Pietie Norval claimed silver in the tennis men's doubles, but Elana Meyer took the headlines.

This small, slight long-distance runner from Stellenbosch was admired and respected, not simply because of her exceptional talent but also because of her quiet, modest manner.

She was everyone's darling and her triumph, finishing second in the women's 10 000m to Derartu Tulu, the phenomenon from Ethiopia, was celebrated by the entire team.

Indeed, the photograph of Elana Meyer and Tulu, two women of Africa, joining hands on their lap of honour set the perfect seal on what, after all, had been a wonderful adventure.

The road to Barcelona may have been paved with uncertainty, haste and conflict but, at least, we returned home smiling.

BUILDING TO ATLANTA

These were important decisions and, as I looked around the NOCSA boardroom, the pressure was beginning to tell. We were dealing in a precious currency; we were dealing in dreams. A large sum of money had been allocated, and applications from our member federations covered the table.

Our task was to decide which athletes would receive special funding as they prepared for the 1996 Olympic Games, and who would not, whose dreams would fly and whose would not.

The challenge for NOCSA was to invest this money in people who would win Olympic medals for South Africa.

This was Operation Excellence in action.

Upon our return from Barcelona in 1992, I had started to plan a talent identification and funding programme where NOCSA could translate its limited funding into visible success. The easy option would have been to divide the money among the federations, and leave them to spend it as they wished, but we could not afford to spread our resources so thinly.

As NOCSA, I strongly believed we should accept responsibility, rather than abdicate it to the federations. We should back our own judgement, and in turn submit ourselves to be judged on South Africa's performance at the next Olympic Games.

My concept was to focus our funding on specific athletes, who had demonstrated genuine potential to succeed. We would identify them, and give them access to the best available coaches, the best available training environments and the best available medical advice. In essence, we would give them the best possible chance to realise their potential.

I drew upon my personal experience of the sports structures deployed in the former East Germany and other Eastern European countries, and from my own interaction with the University sports system in the USA, and devised a programme that would be appropriate to South African society.

On the one hand, the freedom and independent spirit that is rightly encouraged among young South Africans meant few of them would have been prepared to submit their entire lives to the kind of structures that produced medals in East Germany, and other Eastern European countries.

Instructed to jump, young athletes from Leipzig in 1973 would have asked how high, whereas youngsters in Johannesburg 20 years later would have responded by asking why.

Neither approach was right, and neither was wrong, but my planning needed to take into account the reality that, whereas East Germany was a totalitarian country of 17 million people absolutely committed to sports success, South Africa was a democratic country of 42 million who wanted to win, but was not necessarily prepared to exercise the same discipline.

Equally, South Africa clearly did not have the same level of funding available to sport in the United States.

'Operation Excellence' was designed as a hybrid of the world's two best sports systems in modern times, a cross between Berlin and Baltimore that would work well in Bloemfontein.

The first step was to assemble our pool of potential Olympic athletes, and divide them into three clear groups: genuine medal hopes, likely finalists and likely participants.

Detailed applications for specific funding would be submitted by the respective federations, and the NOCSA Committee would be left with awkward choices, for example, between a middle-distance runner and a doubles team in beach volleyball. This was the nature of our task, but there was not enough money for everyone, so tough choices were unavoidable.

So, we sat in the boardroom, in judgement.

As President of Swimming South Africa, I assessed that our women swimmers had real potential. We only had to look at the recent performances of people like Penny Heyns and Marianne Kriel to see that they had become extremely competitive. A detailed discussion followed, which flowed into assessment of what the women's swimming team required.

Jan Bidrman, a top University coach who had represented Czechoslovakia in swimming before defecting to Sweden, was coaching Penny Heyns, and it was clearly in our interest to employ him to work with our entire women's swimming squad on a full-time basis.

We estimated the entire project would cost approximately US$300 000, and the proposal to proceed was fully supported by the Executives of Swimming South Africa and NOCSA.

Then, someone else raised the case of the marathon runners, saying the evidence of recent performances suggested that, on their day, with luck, they could challenge for medals.

"What do they need?"

"The group of four long-distance runners want to spend six weeks at a high-altitude base in Albuquerque, New Mexico, with Jacques Malan employed as their coach."

"How much?"

"Two hundred and fifty thousand dollars."

Again, we analysed expert advice, engaged in careful debate and only then gave approval by general consent.

Somebody asked: "What about Hezekiel Sepeng? He ran well at the IAAF World Championships in Stuttgart."

"What does he need?"

"He has his own coach, but we feel he would benefit if Wilf Paish was employed to look after the whole track and field team, and give some specialist advice to Hezekiel."

"How much?"

"Sixty thousand dollars."

Agreed.

Other decisions followed… to support a training programme in Cape Town, to supplement the income of an athlete in Durban, to pay the travel costs of a gifted athlete who needed experience in Europe.

In the four years prior to the 1996 Olympics in Atlanta, NOCSA invested more than R24 million in Operation Excellence.

This was a substantial amount of money, equivalent to the cost of building four multipurpose sports centres in deprived areas, and some observers did question our strategy.

However, like every other National Olympic Committee around the world, our area of responsibility lay at the elite level, supporting the few men and women whose success will hopefully motivate and inspire the many millions of ordinary participants.

In South Africa, other organisations – such as the National Sports Council (NSC), the Sports Trust and indeed member federations, themselves – accepted the challenge of providing facilities, coaching and equipment at grass roots and schools level.

NOCSA's role within an overall structure, that has evolved and continues to develop, remains to develop elite athletes.

Others must judge how we have performed this role, but my personal view is that we have achieved a great deal in a short space of time and, for this, credit ought to be shared among the team of men and women who built the organisation.

Settling after the blur of Barcelona, we held our first Annual General Meeting in November 1992, where I was elected unopposed as the President of NOCSA, and a proper Executive Committee was democratically elected by the Federations.

Thus, we finally moved beyond where the old organisations occupied entrenched positions on the Executive. Where there had been distrust and suspicion, now there was unity of purpose. Where there had been petty plotting, now there was progress.

Detractors carped from the sidelines that I had brutally taken over and installed my own people, but the Federations had elected both the President and the Executive. Criticism was driven not by fact, but by the embittered envy of the rejected.

Their time had passed.

For us, there was work to be done.

We needed appropriate office space. Ali Bacher had initially accommodated us at the UCB, and we were then offered space at the offices of our travel agents, Fli-Afrika, whose MD, Nazeer Camaroodeen, was always extremely helpful.

Danie Malan, a Vice-President of NOCSA and Director of Sport in Johannesburg, then stepped forward and proved instrumental in resolving what had become an awkward situation.

He had helped us find temporary office space in Main Street, downtown Johannesburg, which we used before Barcelona, but our proper and fitting home was Olympic House, a graceful building set in the northern suburbs parkland of Johannesburg and owned by the City.

The problem was that the former tenants, officials of the establishment white South African National Olympic Committee (SANOC), seemed reluctant to vacate the premises.

Danie was never a man who had difficulty in matching actions with words and, after issuing several warnings, he managed to evict SANOC from Olympic House, and we moved in. He also arranged for NOCSA signboards to be installed at nearby junctions.

In 2002, we expanded the property, constructing a modern office block and completing a fully functional, modern facility that compares favourably with any NOC office worldwide.

In my speech at the opening of the new building, I took care to recall the most important contribution. "Without Danie Malan," I told the audience. "We would not be here today."

We needed a strong Constitution, and I enlisted the help of Krish Naidoo to draft a document that found a delicate balance in giving representation to overwhelmingly white sports federations without completely swamping black participation.

His text also stipulated NOCSA's independence from political interference, confirming our status as an unaligned organisation.

Krish worked diligently and produced a Constitution that, give or take occasional amendments, has stood scrutiny.

We needed to adopt strong business principles throughout the organisation; we needed an effective Secretary-General. In the course of our frenzied exertions in Barcelona, when the staff often needed to work 18 hours a day, I had noticed the superb commitment of one particularly dynamic individual.

Russell Macmillan held a senior position at Sun International at the time, commuting between Johannesburg and Sun City, but he came into our structures through equestrian sport; and, towards the end of the Olympic Games in Barcelona, I asked him if he would be prepared to stand for election as Secretary-General.

He agreed and, over the course of the next four years, made a tremendous contribution to NOCSA at every level, not least by expanding the vocabulary of his colleagues. Barbara Dowell, a prominent school teacher in Durban, served as a representative of South African swimming at the time, and she used to say she wasn't even aware of half the words in the English language till she met Russell.

I recall one meeting when an unlucky delegate was struggling to make his point, as he droned on and on.

After a while, Russell interrupted him, saying softly: "Why don't you just come to the ******* point."

He might have been forthright, but he was highly effective. He had a great ability to make things happen. I was disappointed, but understanding, when he accepted an offer to join the pay-TV channel, Supersport, and had to resign as Secretary-General after just one term.

We also needed financial integrity in all respects and, in this regard, we were privileged to have Kurt Hipper as Treasurer. He was ideal: efficient, rigorous and honest beyond question.

We needed loyal sponsors, and quickly reached a decision to appoint Grinaker Sports Management as our marketing agents. In an industry full of doubtful operators, Clive Grinaker has developed a reputation for innovation, integrity and reliability. We appreciated these qualities as much as the blue-chip companies that he brought to NOCSA as sponsors.

During the period from 1992 to 2004, through many, many presentations and pitches, through a few ups and downs, Clive and his staff brought more than R140 million to NOCSA.

Lastly, we needed sound corporate governance, and this relied upon the quality of person who agreed to serve, unpaid and often unappreciated, on our Executive Committee.

In this respect, NOCSA was very fortunate. Aside from Danie, Russell and Kurt, we drew upon the expertise of Moss Mashishi, who had emerged from the tertiary education sports movement and worked with the NSC.

Dr George van Dugteren (fencing), Ross Robson (sailing), Mluleki George (NSC) and Stan Brickwa (baseball) also joined the Executive.

This was the team, and their input – office space, a strong constitution, business principles, financial integrity, loyal sponsors and corporate governance – resulted in success. Of course, there were moments when things did not progress smoothly, times of frustration and fleeting conflict.

However, in the space of four hectic years, NOCSA developed from not much more than a shell to an established organisation, which, through

Operation Excellence, was capable of providing our Olympic athletes with a genuine winning chance.

This was the new cause. At stages, after returning home from London, I had wondered whether I would ever again feel as motivated and inspired as I had at SANROC, working from a basement office to undermine apartheid in sport, but my new challenge did prove as stimulating.

As a young man, I had always wanted to be involved in sport, and I had only been dragged into the political environment by the circumstances of the time, by the need to oppose apartheid. I didn't regret that reality, but it had not been my choice.

Now, finally, well past my 50th birthday, I was able to fulfil my early ambition, and focus on sport for sport's sake.

I worked hard – devising our structures and systems, getting to know people in our member federations, representing NOCSA in various forums – and I enjoyed myself tremendously.

It soon became clear that the extent of my responsibilities at NOCSA necessitated a full-time, permanent commitment. Elected as President, I was working as an Executive President.

Detractors claimed this was the creation of a dictatorship, but, in fact, my position was consistently monitored and approved by the NOCSA Executive. They recognised my contribution, agreed to pay me a living salary and asked me to keep going.

Invariably arriving in the office before eight in the morning, I rarely got home before eight in the evening. I didn't mind. From my earliest days, I have always wanted to be busy.

Week by week, I became integrated into the new landscape of South African sport, accepted for what I achieved.

The hostility towards me did not completely disappear, but it was generally confined to the extremes of the political spectrum. On the far right, the National Party and Afrikaans newspapers still saw me as a communist politician meddling in sport. On the far left, former members of SACOS resolutely maintained that I had betrayed the cause of nonracial sport by hastening South Africa's readmission to the Olympic arena.

If I had somehow found my way to a point midway between the two, perhaps that wasn't such a terrible thing.

In 1994, to my surprise, and pleasure, I was nominated by the ANC to join the Committee responsible for arranging the historic Inauguration of Nelson Mandela as President.

The country's remarkable negotiated revolution had come to its conclusion with the first democratic elections on April 27th, 1994; these produced a substantial ANC majority, and elected the former prisoner as the first democratically elected leader.

At our first meeting, some officials expressed concern that, on Inauguration Day, too many people would descend upon Pretoria to join the celebrations in the public parks around the Union Buildings, where the new President would take the oath. We clearly needed to create a major Inauguration Day event in Johannesburg that would draw its own large crowd. Aziz Pahad, my colleague on the Committee, and I believed the solution was to stage an international football match in Johannesburg.

Someone asked: "South Africa against who?"

"How about Zambia," Aziz replied.

This proposal was immediately agreed because the symmetry was perfect: most of South Africa's new leaders had been exiled in Lusaka, and this invitation on this special day would recognise the contribution of our comrades to the north.

I was handed the responsibility of organising the match and, working with the South African Football Association, we managed to create an occasion that reflected the joy of thousands of people in the stadium and millions watching on television.

Aziz and I had selected Ellis Park as the venue for the match, in preference to other venues, because that stadium provided the facility of a giant screen that we could use to broadcast events in Pretoria to the spectators at the football match.

South Africa's newly inaugurated President was scheduled to attend the entire match but the celebrations in Pretoria overran and he arrived at Ellis Park just before half-time. We revised our running order, and informed the teams that Mandela would meet the players on the field during the interval.

Once we had reached the podium near the halfway line, I took the microphone and announced: "Ladies and gentlemen, the President of South Africa, Mr Nelson Mandela."

Ellis Park erupted in deafening acclamation, and I reflected on the singular honour of having been the first person to introduce the new President to his own people in a public arena.

In many ways, this extraordinary man proceeded to lead his united but fragile country by sheer force of personality.

Through uncertain times, when so many people's lives were changing so dramatically, he smiled, found the right words and persuaded them everything will be all right.

Through angry times, when revenge and conflict appeared to be inevitable, he embraced even those who had persecuted him and grew to exemplify grace, peace and reconciliation. In the most critical period of our history, Mandela showed all South Africans how they could be, how they could forgive, unite and grow together. Enough of his compatriots liked what they saw, and copied him for the miraculous transition to unfold.

He defined the 1995 Rugby World Cup, the first major sports event to be hosted in South Africa, by wearing a No 6 Springbok jersey and cap onto the field before the final, and the nation united to celebrate the country's first World Champions. Nine months later, he defined the 1996 African Cup of Nations when he beamed and danced on the field after Bafana Bafana, the South African national side, had beaten Tunisia in the final.

He led; the rest of us followed.

It was, therefore, significant to me when this iconic figure found the time to recognise my own personal achievement in June 1995, when I was elected to become a Member of the International Olympic Committee at the IOC Session in Budapest.

"Dear Sam," he wrote. "On behalf of the government and all South Africans, my heartiest congratulations to you on your election to the General Assembly of the IOC. This honour represents another milestone for sport in South Africa.

"You have, over the years, established yourself as a highly competent sports administrator and you are well equipped to take up this responsibility."

I was naturally pleased to accept membership of the IOC, an organisation that I had observed at close quarters for more than 20 years, not least because it enabled me to represent South Africa in the highest, most influential forum of world sport.

IOC members take their seats at each session in order of their election, so I sat nearby Valeriy Borzov, the Ukrainian sprinter who I had so admired when, representing the USSR, he won the 100m and 200m sprint double at the 1972 Olympics, and next to Jean-Claude Killy, the French ski champion who won three gold medals at the Winter Olympic Games in 1968.

Humbled by such exalted company, I quietly resolved to work hard for the Olympic movement, to protect and project its ideals and to represent my country with distinction.

"Lofty ideals," cynics will say, but they meant a great deal to me on the day I was appointed, and they still do.

So, in every way, at both a national and personal level, we approached the 1996 Olympic Games with optimism.

South African sport was in buoyant mood: the rugby team were world champions, the football side were champions of Africa, and the cricketers had recently defeated England. The sporting public were growing accustomed to a regular diet of glory and triumph, and they expected nothing less than medals from the athletes preparing to compete in Atlanta.

We were expected to deliver, and, having flown to the United States in a specially painted South African Airways jumbo jet, named Ndizane (a Zulu word meaning 'soaring to the heights'), our athletes certainly did deliver.

Penny Heyns was first to strike gold, and create history. No South African had ever won two gold medals at the same Olympics, until she did. No woman had ever won both the 100m and 200m breaststroke races in the same Games, until she did.

I felt a special affinity with this committed, admirable woman, not simply because I was President of Swimming South Africa, and she was catapulting our code into the headlines at home, but also because we had backed her ever since 1992. Back then, trying to qualify for Barcelona, she set the fastest time in the heats but finished second in the final. In what became a controversial, much criticised decision, we opted to include Penny in the team, ahead of Sheila Turner, who won the final.

Our justification was that Penny had posted the fastest time, but our instinct was, with the benefit of Olympic experience in 1992, she would be a genuine medal prospect four years later.

She proceeded to join a strong swimming programme at the University of Nebraska, developed into a true world-class swimmer and unforgettably rose to the occasion in Atlanta.

As South Africans, we were enjoying ourselves at the Olympic pool and our rainbow flag was soon being hoisted again.

Marianne Kriel produced a fantastic swim to claim a bronze medal in the 100m backstroke, and our women's four x 100m relay team brought us to our feet, and finished fourth.

It was appropriate that Thabo Mbeki, Zanele Mbeki, Essop Pahad and Steve Tshwete were all present at the Olympic pool that day and they joined in our celebrations.

Penny, Marianne and their colleagues in the relay team had all attended the pre-Games training camp in Nebraska, made possible by NOCSA's Operation Excellence. As we celebrated their medals, the Executive reflected upon US$ 300,000 well spent.

Several days later, Hezekiel Sepeng ran strongly in the heats and secured his place in the 800m final. Now we wondered how this hugely talented, likeable young man from Potchefstroom would respond to the unique pressure of an Olympic final.

In the event, he produced a heroic burst in the home straight and crossed the finish line, eyes blazing and arms aloft, in the silver medal position.

Again, members of the NOCSA Executive were able to glance at each other in the stand and smile because their investment in Wilf Paish, to direct our athletes and assist JP van der Merwe in the coaching of Sepeng, had yielded a silver dividend.

Helga and I watched the start of the marathon on television in our Atlanta hotel room. We knew our team had potential, but it was always difficult to predict success over 42km.

Barely an hour later, we walked into a street near the hotel and watched the leading runners past the 20km mark. All three South Africans were in touch, in contention.

"Maybe they have a chance," Helga said.

"I think we had better rush to the stadium," I replied.

I have never been somebody who cries easily. Even as a boy in Magazine Barracks, in Durban, I very rarely wept at anything. It just wasn't done. That wasn't the way we were raised. However, there were tears gathering in my eyes when Josiah Thugwane, a mineworker from Mpumalanga, ran into the Olympic Stadium at Atlanta, leading the men's marathon.

He ran the last two and half circuits of the track, won the race and humbly accepted the applause of the crowd. NOCSA had spent a quarter of a million dollars on the marathon squad's training camp in Albuquerque, and Josiah had just said thank you.

The 1996 Olympic Games may have been criticised by many observers, mainly for an unwieldy transport system, but the South African team had enjoyed themselves in Atlanta.

They arrived home to a heroes' reception with a collective five medals, three of which were gold. By general consent, the team had excelled at the most competitive level of international sport and, in so doing, sustained the country's winning run.

Penny, Marianne, Hezekiel and Josiah were quickly placed on pedestals as bold symbols of the new South Africa. Two women and two men, two whites and two blacks: they might have been chosen by a marketing guru for a television commercial.

In fact, of course, the quartet of Olympic medallists became NOCSA's commercial: living, winning evidence of what could be achieved by talent, courage and proper funding.

Each of them became an outstanding ambassador for South Africa around the world, and for the Olympic movement within their own country. Their names will never be forgotten.

Correctly, the athletes received the glory and recognition, but it was important for us, the NOCSA Executive, to recognise that our Operation Excellence had delivered the results.

Of course, we had also invested in several other athletes, who did not perform so well at the Olympics in Atlanta.

However, as a group, we had sat in that boardroom and made the tough decisions, and been rewarded by five gleaming, prized pieces of metal ware: three gold, one silver and one bronze.

OLYMPIC CHALLENGE

Excited by their Olympic experience in Atlanta, many South Africans began to dream of hosting the Games on our own soil. It was a wonderful prospect. Cape Town had put itself forward as a candidate city to stage the Olympic Games of 2004, and was proposing that Africa's time had come to host its first Olympics.

Our athletes' success in Atlanta brought momentum to the bid and, given South Africa's remarkable and wonderful capacity to get excited, CT2004 was soon flying; or so it seemed.

In fact, within the IOC, Athens was always the overwhelming favourite to host the Games in 2004, simply by virtue of the fact that many members believed the Greek capital should have won the right to host the event in 1996, and this was payback.

Back then, the IOC had selected the stronger commercial environment of Atlanta, overlooking the Athens campaign to take the Olympics back to its ancient origins.

In this contest, more than any other, past suffering can be a passport to success. So, Athens banked the sympathy in the race for 1996 and cantered to victory eight years later.

These factors lay far beyond the control of anybody in Cape Town, and they should not detract from a gallant and courageous Olympic bid that was, in many respects, a success. The city reached the final shortlist of five, and third place, behind Athens, the winners, and Rome, but ahead of Stockholm and Buenos Aires, represented a creditable result, casting Cape Town as a desirable destination on the global stage.

The bid also captured the public imagination for a while and, most importantly, established expertise that served the country well in future campaigns to host major sports events. Many key figures in South Africa's successful bid to stage the 2010 FIFA World Cup gained their first experience of international bidding as members of the Cape Town 2004 team.

Having said all this, any successful Olympic bid demands total trust and harmony between four key groups: Government, at central and provincial level, the City Council, the National Olympic Committee and the Bid.

Cape Town 2004 failed to meet this requirement; indeed, the Bid was notable for its infighting, and almost everybody has their own explanation and their own people to blame.

My personal view is that the dominant personalities within the Bid, first Raymond Ackerman, then Chris Ball, were both forthright, over-confident, white businessmen who, in fact, understood neither the dynamics of unified South African sport nor the mechanism and customs of the International Olympic Committee.

Both brought some talents to the Bid, and maybe both arrived with the best intentions, but, in the end, first Ackerman and then Ball appeared to believe humility was a weakness. In fact, it was a necessity.

Under Ackerman, the Cape Town 2004 Bid Company generally treated central government, the City Council and NOCSA with disdain.

In his mind, the Councillors were not elected leaders who best understood the mentality and potential of their city… my impression was that he seemed to think they were just a bunch of second-rate, meddling politicians.

In his mind, NOCSA was not the body best placed to judge the mood of the IOC and influence its members… my impression was that he seemed to think it was a ramshackle group.

The Bid, apparently, was the fountain of all knowledge. This lion of the corporate jungle thought he knew it all, and treated the rest of us with contempt. As a result, there was no trust and the Bid was riddled with infighting.

It was Ackerman who first conceived and drove the dream of Cape Town hosting the Olympic Games. Following an internal domestic contest, the NOCSA Executive and our advisors decided Cape Town had a better chance of winning the bid than Durban or Johannesburg.

The supermarket tycoon seemed set on running the bid as an extracurricular activity of his vast corporate empire, for the glory of Cape Town and, of course, for himself as well. Sadly, he didn't appreciate the complexities of the challenge, and seemed unused to accepting advice from anyone.

When he should have been trying to build a consensus among all the diverse communities in Cape Town, he issued edicts from his office and appeared astonishingly oblivious to the mood and spirit of the new South Africa where people were no longer prepared to bow and grovel at the feet of the big, white boss.

As President of NOCSA, I felt obliged to meet Ackerman and suggest that he involve the City of Cape Town in the bid. Needless to say, he didn't appreciate my intervention. He didn't like me then, and he has waged a personal vendetta ever since.

That is his right, of course, but I do not subscribe to the view that a personality clash developed between us. We simply did not agree on how to structure the Cape Town bid: I believed we needed to establish an inclusive, trusting partnership between the Bid, the City, the Government and NOCSA, and, essentially, he wanted to do everything on his own.

Conflict was inevitable.

Eventually, when it became clear we would not play according to his rules, Ackerman took his ball and went home. He did not leave the Bid quietly, and promptly deployed his highly skilled, highly paid publicity department to generate negative publicity for those who had confronted him.

I became the target of heavy criticism in the media, but opted to say nothing in response, for fear of provoking further conflict and causing more collateral damage to the bid. This had always been my reaction: don't get involved, keep a bit of dignity and wait for the hostility to blow over.

This may well have been right strategy for the bid, but it was wrong for me because a series of falsehoods were allowed to pass unchallenged into general acceptance. Even today, I still bear some of the scars of Ackerman's vindictive and sustained onslaught.

His departure created an opportunity to revive and reshape the bid. Steve Tshwete, Minister of Sport and Recreation, became the new Chairman, with NOCSA Vice-President Danie Malan as his deputy and, in due course, Chris Ball, a former banker, was appointed as CEO. The City was properly included, and we made progress.

Relations within the Bid never became ideal, and certain IOC members from Africa continued to express reservations that too many of the people leading our bid were white and, so, did not explicitly represent Africa.

However, President Mandela fully committed himself to the campaign, and his plea on behalf of Africa struck a chord. I also worked hard to lobby within the IOC and Ball deserves credit for directing a capable bid that was not disgraced when the IOC members cast their votes in Lausanne.

On that day, remarkably, more than 30 000 Capetonians gathered at Grand Parade in the city centre to watch the IOC announcement on a giant screen, wildly optimistic that their city, their country and their President would somehow prevail.

The disappointment at the final decision was palpable and, in the months that followed, many questioned the point of any South African city bidding to host the Games ever again.

Time has healed, and the South African Football Association's success in winning the right to host the FIFA World Cup in 2010 has once again prompted excited discussion about a South African city making a fresh Olympic bid in the near future.

I believe we should certainly bid again, but South Africa must approach such a contest with the same patience and realism that one of our greatest sporting rivals showed in the recent past.

The Australians decided they wanted to host the Olympics, so they bid to stage the 1992 Games in Brisbane, but lost. Undeterred by defeat, they bid for 1996 with Melbourne, and lost again. Still resolved, they bid for 2000 with Sydney, and won.

Very few cities bid for the first time, and win. So long as every stakeholder understands we may well bid and lose again before we bid and win, of course we should pursue the dream.

There is a common suggestion that I have insisted Johannesburg must be the next South African city to prepare a bid. This is not true.

I believe Cape Town, Durban and Johannesburg all have the infrastructure and capacity to stage a successful Games; it is simply essential that any future bid is based on harmonious relationships between the three key stakeholders: Government at all levels, the City Council and NOCSA.

If everyone is pulling in the same direction, and nobody is worrying who takes the credit, it is very possible that the Olympics could come to South Africa within the next 16 years.

NOCSA had ploughed on through the strain of the Cape Town bid, an exercise that incidentally left us with a substantial expense, and began to prepare for the 2000 Olympics in Sydney.

We had become a robust, confident organisation and, in the months preceding the 2000 Olympics, we needed all our strength to withstand a wildly overblown selection controversy.

The bare facts are these: the largely white men's hockey side qualified to compete in Sydney, but the NOCSA Executive refused to include them in the South African Olympic team, which did contain the largely multiracial national baseball side.

"That's racist," the local hockey community complained, in its disappointment. "It's apartheid in reverse."

They duly protested to the International Hockey Federation, as they were perfectly entitled to do, and the IHF took their case to the IOC, who eventually ruled in NOCSA's favour.

That should have been the end of the matter. Instead, a few hockey officials and players pursued their resentment in the media, attacking NOCSA relentlessly, and me personally, and engulfing our entire Olympic campaign in bitterness and controversy.

At first glance, maybe the hockey caucus had a point. 'White hockey team left behind, multiracial baseball side selected': to the casual observer, the NOCSA decision did seem unfair.

In reality, it was no more than the logical implementation of an absolutely transparent NOCSA selection policy, which had been tabled, discussed and agreed by the federations.

This is the background.

Following unity and readmission, most South African sporting codes faced exactly the same challenge: to produce national teams that represented the demography of the new democracy. Bluntly, it was considered necessary to increase black representation without removing merit selection and alienating whites.

A balancing act was required, and some high-profile sports chose to deal with the matter shadily, indistinctly. Affirmative action became the policy that dare not speak its name.

One young white cricketer was selected in the South African Test team, only to be replaced by a black player on the morning of the match. Nobody said anything, although it was later reported that the United Cricket Board officials had intervened because they refused to accept an 'all-white' side.

Similarly, a white winger was rumoured to have been included in the Springbok rugby team but then suddenly withdrawn two days before a Test, and abruptly replaced with a black teammate.

Again there was no official statement, but rumours circulated that the South African Rugby Football Union had adopted an unspoken rule that no Springbok team would take the field without a certain number of black players in the side and a certain number of black players on the bench.

Such erratic, undercover commotion appeared an inadequate response to the matter, because nobody knew where they stood, team morale was eroded and the players concerned were placed in an almost impossible situation.

At NOCSA, we decided to confront the challenge by formulating, declaring and implementing an open, honest selection policy.

Our task was clear: to produce an Olympic team which was affordable in terms of size, and which properly represented the new South Africa even though many of our member federations, like canoeing, sailing, shooting, swimming, hockey and others, were historically dominated by whites.

We adopted a scientific approach, and produced a two-tiered plan that has been praised and copied around the world.

First, we unequivocally declared that any athlete or team with a realistic chance of winning a medal would be placed on the upper tier, which meant being included in the team and, where possible, being funded and supported by Operation Excellence, the programme for high-performance athletes.

In most countries, this is the only criterion for selection: if you can win, we take you. If not, you watch on television.

At NOCSA, we wanted to do better than that, so we decided to create a second tier in our Olympic team where we would be able to (a) foster developing talent, and (b) address the inequity of our past by creating opportunities both for previously disadvantaged black athletes and for teams that, through development, included a significant proportion of black players.

In this way, we believed we could assemble an Olympic team that reflected the IOC's proclaimed ideals of quality and universality, blending the principle of merit selection on the upper tier and a sincere commitment to develop young and historically denied talent on the second tier.

We never claimed the policy was perfect because terms like 'previously disadvantaged' are too often ill-defined, but we believed it offered the best solution to our challenge and would enable us to select a competitive and truly representative team.

All seemed well.

Problems arose when white South African athletes and largely white South African teams began to qualify for the Olympics in the sports, like fencing, table tennis, rowing, hockey and the rest, that remained largely undeveloped in the rest of Africa.

They would return home brandishing gold medals from their respective African Championships and look forward to competing at the Olympics. However, in many cases, to their disappointment, they did not meet our agreed criteria for selection.

It was impossible for us to include them on the upper tier because, even if they were the best in Africa, they evidently stood no realistic chance of winning an Olympic medal, or even reaching the final.

And they could not qualify for the second tier unless they were a 'previously disadvantaged' individual or they were a team that included 'previously disadvantaged' players, as this category catered for development.

Thus, the men's hockey side could not be selected in the team for the Olympics of 2000: even though they had qualified through Africa, they stood no real chance of winning a medal in Sydney and they did not include a significant number of previously disadvantaged players in their squad.

Other individuals and teams, like several gymnasts and the fencing squad, also qualified through Africa but were not selected, yet they recognised NOCSA was not making a racial judgement and calmly accepted the application of an agreed selection policy.

The national baseball team was selected for Sydney because, even though they had also qualified in Africa, a strong development programme meant they did include a significant number of previously disadvantaged players.

One hockey official then asked: "So, if we put some blacks in the team, would you let us compete in Sydney?"

In more than 40 years of working in sport, I don't believe any remark has left me feeling so infuriated and disheartened.

Many people had sacrificed their lives to oppose apartheid and create the democratic conditions that meant this particular official could even consider participating at the Olympics.

Even at my level, I had suffered two decades of exile and separation from my family, persecution and bullets in the bedroom wall. Yet, I had endured and campaigned because I believed in the cause of equal opportunities in South African sport.

Now, as we worked hard to reconcile and devise a policy that would both preserve merit selection and create equal opportunities through sincere development, this individual was looking me in the eye and scornfully suggesting I should be satisfied by the cynical, cosmetic selection of a few hapless stooges.

I replied: "We do not subscribe to tokenism."

The two-tiered NOCSA selection policy remains in force to this day and, by general consent, it represents one of the most honest and transparent transformation strategies in sport.

So, the 127 members of the South African Olympic team of 2000 assembled, not in smiling unity, but in an atmosphere clouded and poisoned by the hockey-fuelled controversy.

Unfortunately, I believe this negative vibe ultimately coloured the popular judgement of the team's performance.

Our critics focused on the reality that we failed to win a single gold medal in Sydney, and seized on that statistic to criticise NOCSA and launch yet another media offensive against me.

In the process, they cynically undermined what was, by any objective analysis, an excellent team achievement.

Hestrie Cloete (silver, women's high jump), Terence Parkin (silver, 200m breaststroke), Frantz Kruger (bronze, discus), Penny Heyns (bronze, 100m breaststroke) and Llewellyn Herbert (bronze, 400m hurdles) all deserved a much better reception.

South Africa won a total of five medals in Sydney, equal to the five we won in Atlanta, and our athletes reached 28 finals in what is the most intensely competitive arena in world sport.

We were one of only 70 countries to win medals, and one of just 41 to take home five or more. Comparable African nations, like Nigeria, who won three silver, and Egypt, who won nothing at all, would have celebrated an equivalent performance.

The magazine, *Competition Sport*, conducts an in-depth study into each country's performance at the Olympics. Giving nine points for gold, seven for silver, six for bronze right down to one for a place in the final, they produce a cumulative points table that provides a more scientific gauge than the simple medal table.

In the *Competition Sport* league, South Africa was ranked 46th at Barcelona in 1992, 33rd at Atlanta in 1996 and then improved its position to a respectable 27th at Sydney in 2000.

Emerging from an era when most of our athletes were denied an equal opportunity, we have excelled.

In future, as the normalisation process continues, and is one day completed, I believe South Africans can expect their team to be regularly ranked among the top 25 Olympic nations at the summer Games. We will continue to compete at the Winter Olympics, but our ambitions shall obviously be more modest.

This would reflect the status of a strong sporting country with reasonable, but not exceptional, resources, ready and eager to play a constructive role within the Olympic movement.

Such standing will not be secured without the dedication of the athletes, across the country, in every sport, the federations and NOCSA, and it will also require substantial financial investment, but I believe these sacrifices will be worthwhile.

For the Olympic Games continues to represent the very best of humankind, a uniquely simple arena of competition, untainted by prize money and brash commercial branding.

Recent research suggested that the Olympic logo, the interlocking rings representing the five continents, has become the most recognised and identified symbol on the planet.

For 16 days, every four years, the entire world focuses on one chosen city and, through the skill and courage of the athletes, shares in an uplifting celebration of unity and peace.

It is the responsibility of the IOC, of which I am a member, to protect and preside over this valuable institution, and everything I see and hear at Sessions and Commission meetings throughout the year suggests the movement is in sound health.

The image of IOC members as lavish fat cats is far removed from the reality of many decent people working extremely hard for the benefit of Olympism and sport in general.

In 2001, Jacques Rogge, of Belgium, was elected as the new IOC President, and his determination to democratise every area of the organisation has been universally welcomed.

The curse of corruption has been addressed and, while nobody denies the IOC's reputation was damaged by recent corruption scandals, codes of conduct have been tightened and the procedure for candidate cities bidding to stage the Games, too often abused in the past, has been reviewed and streamlined. In the process, the IOC has effectively set the stage for other major sports organisations to follow suit.

Drugs have also threatened to undermine the integrity of the Games but, again, rigorously updated testing procedures have been introduced to catch the cheats, and, by general consent, the Games are now cleaner than for a generation.

There is no complacency on either front but, under Rogge's firm hand, the IOC appears to be winning the wars on corruption and drugs, creating time to discuss other issues.

In my view, the paramount challenge facing the movement is to contain the scale of the summer Olympics, to prevent the event from becoming too large, expensive and cumbersome.

Recent Games have been restricted to 28 sporting codes, but there is a growing opinion that the size of the event would be better controlled by imposing a limit of 10 500 athletes, and removing any hard and fast maximum number of sports.

Such a decision would create an opportunity for currently favoured sports such as rugby and golf to be included in the schedule by 2012.

Whatever is decided, I am sure the Olympic movement will continue to evolve and, as long as I am spared, I will eagerly contribute to the debate and assist in effecting the necessary changes until the day when I retire.

NOCSA CHALLENGE

When somebody said I ran NOCSA like a corner shop, I was happy to accept the remark as a compliment. In my view, it is important to know exactly what is happening, to be involved in every activity, to be frugal and live within your means, to recognise every item on the balance sheet.

These have been important principles in the 12 years that I have served, unopposed, as President of NOCSA.

Indeed, reflecting on that period, the realisation of financial security has been one of our major achievements, and the 'corner shop' philosophy has, in fact, served us well.

During my time at SANROC, there was no option. We had so few resources that, when we travelled to attend a congress or an event, we always tried to stay with friends or, failing that, we would find a small bed-and-breakfast establishment; and we were always conscious of eating as cheaply as possible.

Every year, as a firm rule, I drew up the SANROC annual budget to make a surplus, even if this usually meant we had to cut expenditure to the bone, often into the bone.

I suppose it was only natural that I should carry this mentality into NOCSA, and, over the years, I have tried to instil a culture of thrift and frugality throughout the organisation.

When I travel to Cape Town on NOCSA business, rather than hire a car, I ask colleagues to meet me at the airport, take me to the meeting and then drop me back afterwards.

If it's absolutely necessary to spend a night away from home, then I stay at a Holiday Inn, where we pay special rates from the Southern Sun hotel group, one of our suppliers.

In 12 years since our formation in 1992, it is a matter of pride that we have never been overdrawn at the bank.

We work on four-year cycles and, since we receive the bulk of our income in the latter half of the quadrennial, we have always followed a cautious policy of keeping a reasonable reserve in the bank, to ensure our activities are always funded.

Approximately 70 percent of NOCSA's income is derived from our well-maintained commercial programme, a further 20 percent from the IOC Worldwide Sponsorship Programme, which distributes grants to various NOCs, and only 10 percent from Government.

This breakdown makes us the exception in Africa, where most National Olympic Committees, even those in comparable countries like Egypt, Nigeria and Kenya, are largely funded by Government.

Clearly, we have received extraordinary support from our commercial partners, both those companies who have supported us in the past, notably Nedbank and Volkswagen, and our current cluster – Vodacom, DaimlerChrysler, Sasol, Telkom, South African Airways, Adidas and the South African Broadcasting Corporation.

I hope that we, in return, have delivered an excellent return on their substantial and continuing investment.

Vodacom is our most long-standing sponsor because, I like to believe, the company understands exactly what NOCSA is trying to achieve under the slogan 'Making Greater South Africans'. It might sound like a throwaway line in a press release, but Vodacom, and particularly CEO Alan Knott-Craig, have truly shared our vision almost from our first day of existence.

Our association has been exemplary, maturing to a point where they have faith in us to run our organisation effectively and, in the process, provide a return on their investment.

When, in the weeks preceding the Olympic Games in Sydney, we believed it was necessary to launch an incentive scheme for our athletes, Vodacom stepped forward to support us.

We met and discussed the detail – agreeing gold medallists would receive R1 000 000, silver medallists would get R500 000 and bronze medallists R250 000 – and the deal was done.

Our other main achievement over the past 12 years has been to establish a solid administrative structure, which is clearly defined within the landscape of South African sport.

I am aware that, at various stages, people inside and outside NOCSA have construed my willingness to be concerned with almost every aspect of our activities as unnecessary.

They have suggested that, as President, I should more often be prepared to stand back and focus on the big picture, developing strategy and policy rather than dabbling in detail, worrying about expenses or the latest distorted newspaper report.

In some ways, they could be right but I would not accept that my hands-on attitude makes me either autocratic or dictatorial. On the contrary, I firmly believe in corporate governance, as members of the NOCSA Executive would surely confirm.

That said, like anyone else, I am a product of my background. If there is a rand to be saved, I will save it because, for most of my life, money has been scarce. If there is a job to be done, I will do it because, for much of my life, I have worked alone.

That is my way. I like to lead from the front, and I prefer my lieutenants to stand behind me, not ahead of me.

On reflection, I believe this attentive, firm style of leadership has suited NOCSA during this recent period of transition.

Aside from the major challenge of forging unity of purpose among 31 diverse Olympic Federations and many others, we have also had to fight for our role within the general South African sports structure.

Often rolling with the ebb and flow of government policy, we have clearly stated our role as the sole governing body of Olympic sport in this country, and stood our ground.

When the National Sports Council became responsible for development programmes and organising the South African team at the Commonwealth Games, we retained our role.

When the NSC evolved into the Sports Commission, bringing new definitions and responsibilities, we engaged and contributed to the debate, always protecting our core function.

In boardrooms and at conferences, we have been challenged and tested, but we have held firm and emerged as an unequivocally defined, effective organisation, uniformly respected by our athletes and federations and by every level of government.

Not long after the Olympic Games in Sydney, members of the Executive told me I was doing too much. I accepted their advice, and we set about finding a Chief Executive Officer.

Our search settled on a person who was then working at a bank. He committed himself to the task well, but didn't settle and eventually resigned in April 2004.

Nonetheless, I still believe an organisation as large as NOCSA needs a President and a full-time CEO, ideally a person with business acumen and a sporting background.

The CEO does have to deal with large sums of money and nurture relationships with our commercial partners but, above all, he must earn the respect of our member federations.

However, the task of finding a CEO will not be mine.

As long ago as 2000, after discussing the matter with my wife, I reached the firm decision that I would stand down as President of NOCSA after the 2004 Olympic Games in Athens.

By then, I will have served three full terms, thrice unopposed, and it will be time for new blood and fresh ideas.

It will, of course, be for others to stand in judgement of my overall contribution to NOCSA. However, humbly, I hope I can leave, as a legacy, a sound financial and administrative structure.

Looking forward, NOCSA's paramount challenge is to continue and accelerate the process of transformation, to ensure our Olympic team more accurately represents our young democracy.

We have made substantial progress in the past 12 years. The South African team at Barcelona 1992 included only a handful of black athletes, but more than 30 percent of our team at the 2004 Olympic Games in Athens will be 'previously disadvantaged'.

I believe it is reasonable to expect parity, a 50-50 ratio, in the South African Olympic team that competes in 2012.

This steady development is partly explained by application of a two-tiered selection policy, outlined in the previous chapter, but it also reflects the commitment of our federations.

Sports such as canoeing, gymnastics and many others have been almost exclusively played by whites for more than a century, but hundreds of administrators and coaches, at every level, have shown a missionary zeal to broaden the base of these Olympic sports.

The late Des Park, formerly Secretary and President of the South African Canoeing Association, perfectly demonstrated what can be achieved in this area, and the emergence of a talented crop of young, black canoeists is his proud legacy.

Our federations are sincere in wanting to introduce their sport to their previously disadvantaged compatriots, to launch audacious coaching programmes in the townships but, usually, such dreams are tethered to the ground by a lack of funds.

It is a simple fact that, in South Africa, many Olympic sports scarcely appear on the public awareness radar alongside the giants of football, cricket and rugby, and it becomes impossible for them to secure a share of sponsors or media exposure.

In most cases, participation in these sports is only sustained by the willingness of athletes themselves, administrators and often their parents, to dip into their own pockets and meet the costs.

Against this background, it is impractical and unreasonable to expect federations to fund what are necessarily expensive development programmes from their own meagre resources.

What is the solution?

Only central Government can make a difference. Ultimately, the Department of Sport and Recreation should be empowered to create a collective fund, earmarked to facilitate transformation in the Olympic codes often referred to as 'minor' sports.

I realise Government has many other priorities, and nobody would be happier than me if such an ambitious programme could be viably funded from sponsors or external source. But, for the sake of the federations, I hope good news is not long coming.

There is so much sporting talent in the townships, and money spent unleashing and maximising that raw potential, creating new heroes, inspiring the youth, must be money well spent.

And the return on this investment will be much more than just a few warm, fuzzy feelings on a Saturday afternoon.

Sport has become increasingly relevant. Where once it was regarded as fun and games, it has now become an important factor in any country's international status and standing.

Perceptibly or imperceptibly, nations that perform well at the major international sports events rise in the global pecking order, attracting attention, admiration and investment.

Australia is an example of a country that, since 1980, has spent hundreds of millions of dollars on sport, funding several of the most technically advanced training programmes in the world and creating a genuinely world-class infrastructure.

The return on this investment has been victory after victory, an excellent record in international sport, regular boosts to national morale and global status as a 'winning nation'.

This success has trickled down into tourism, other forms of investment, economic growth, jobs and prosperity.

Today, it is difficult to find a single Australian who does not agree the investment in sport was not worthwhile.

Of course, different priorities exist in South Africa – there are many historic imbalances to be redressed – but there is no doubt that we share the natural sporting ability and commitment to match Australia's achievement, and emulate her success.

The taps are waiting to be turned.

I hope I live to see the day when all South African athletes are empowered to realise their potential, and take on the world.

NOT DONE YET

Peeople tell me retirement is all right as long as you have a good job to go to. When I step down as President of NOCSA in November 2004, I certainly don't intend to stop working. There must always be a purpose in life, right through until your dying day. As the IOC member in SA, I will retain a seat on the NOCSA Executive, but there will be no backseat driving. The new leadership will direct the organisation as they see fit, and they will be assured of my support as and when required.

My ongoing responsibilities as a Member of the International Olympic Committee, and various IOC Commissions, will continue to take time, and I will remain involved in swimming administration, at both an international and a national level.

These are exciting times for swimming and, as a member of the FINA Bureau, the world governing body, I will continue to make a contribution. The struggle against doping is ongoing and serious but, with superstars like Ian Thorpe and Michael Phelps breaking world records, exhilarating crowds and creating headlines, international swimming is enjoying a golden era.

I served as President of Swimming South Africa from 1991 to 1996, and as Deputy President ever since. Our swimmers have obviously performed exceptionally well, and I believe they will continue to provide a source of medals at major events.

In the future, in some capacity, I hope to assist South African swimming in its major challenge to increase black participation, not only in terms of producing top-class competitors but also to raise general awareness of staying safe in water. The diary will be full.

Beyond sport, I would also like to make a contribution in other fields, perhaps conservation, environment or tourism.

The Minister of Tourism and the Environment appointed me as an Ambassador of South African Tourism in September 1998, and I look forward to having the time to fulfil my various responsibilities more diligently.

I hope to spend far more time with my wife, Helga, than has been possible in recent years. We have talked about travelling to India, where we would like to explore the region from where my grandparents originated.

Sitting here in my office at Olympic House, to my right, there is a wall full of certificates and awards. Each one sparks memories of a special day or a particular time of my life. I sincerely appreciate such recognition, since they somehow seem to represent verification of a worthwhile life in sport and society, and yet, for me, the real rewards are the remarkable scenes that regularly unfold before my eyes almost every single day.

Not long ago I was waiting in a queue at a domestic check-in desk at Johannesburg Airport, and a school party passed by. I have no idea where they were going, but these children, aged ten or eleven, were chattering and clearly very excited.

It struck me that perhaps a third of them were white, and the rest were black, but it certainly did not seem to strike them. These were new South Africans, utterly at peace with each other, oblivious to the differences that divided their parents. They will only know of apartheid what they have to read in history books.

Now, I am not a romantic by nature and I am very well aware of the major challenges that confront our country, but, as someone who vividly recalls a bitter past, this scene of harmony did serve to remind me how far we have all come. If the sacrifices that I have made during my life contributed in some small way to the creation of the democratic, optimistic and peaceful country where those children can be so happy and relaxed together, then I do feel a degree of satisfaction.

The reconciliation that has taken place within South Africa over the past 15 years has been truly remarkable, and the highly successful 2003 Cricket World Cup offered another opportunity for the country to show its rainbow face to the world. Attending the final, I sat beside one of the legends of West Indian cricket, Sir Evaton Weekes, and he told me how he had once worked with the Anti-Apartheid Movement in the Caribbean.

He recalled the situation that arose in 1981, when Guyana refused entry to Robin Jackman, a member of the English touring squad, because he had played in South Africa. Matches had to be cancelled, he said.

"People made real sacrifices on behalf of the struggle against apartheid,"

Sir Evaton continued. "So it is surprising for me to visit South Africa all these years later and find that the selfsame Robin Jackman is now one of your TV commentators. Good luck to him. It just strikes me as strange."

I listened carefully.

His comments prompted me to wonder whether there ought to be any limit to reconciliation, any process by which those people who fought apartheid are given priority over those who collaborated. On the other hand, perhaps the essence of reconciliation is that there is no limit, that nobody is ever beyond the pale, whatever they have done.

Certainly, Sir Evaton's point echoes the sentiments of many people from within the former nonracial sports movement who still maintain far too much was conceded too quickly.

"We endured so much for so long," they say, "and now, to a large extent, we sit back and allow most of the sports people who oppressed us to carry on as if nothing ever happened. What has really changed? What have the black, Coloured and Indian sports communities really gained from unification except for a few seats on the Board and the odd facility?"

I understand such opinions, but I do not share them because, in my view, the end justified the means. We sacrificed so much that if we had to sacrifice an element of retribution as well, to build the kind of country we have today, then so be it.

It is now our responsibility, as representatives of the former nonracial sports movement, to use our positions on the various Executives to ensure that proper development programmes are put in place, that real, lasting change is implemented, that every South African does, in fact, have an equal opportunity in sport. I frequently stress to my colleagues that it is more important to see demographic representation on the playing field than in the boardroom.

We may not have completely achieved that goal during the unity negotiations, but we have the capacity to make it happen now.

Within the wider transformation process, there is no doubt that the Truth and Reconciliation Commission played an important role in helping the country move on from apartheid. The process where various people confessed to their past actions and applied for amnesty may have been harrowing and painful, but it drew a line beneath the past.

Dougie Oakes, a journalist who worked in the London office of the South African Argus group, revealed how his Bureau Chief gave him strict instructions that every time he quoted me in an article, he must also secure a counter-quote from the pro-South African Fairness in Sport Organisation.

This small but telling insight prompted me to wonder whether a sporting Truth and Reconciliation Commission might have proved an extremely worthwhile exercise for all involved.

Of course, it would not have dealt with matters as severe as covert police activity, murder and massacre, but such a process might have helped sports people come to terms with the bitterly divided past from which we were compelled by circumstance to rush so quickly into unification and readmission.

Certainly, someone like Sir Evaton Weekes would have been interested to hear someone like Robin Jackman give testimony, to learn whether the cricketer regretted his actions at all.

In any event, South Africans have lived through a miraculous transition and, after 10 years of democracy, we can now reflect that the political transformation is substantially settled. The task for the next decade is to accelerate the pace of social and economic reform, to manage the transformation of South African society and effectively eradicate poverty in all its forms.

As we found a leader to guide us through the initial challenge, so I am convinced we have a leader to guide us now.

In times to come, historians will reflect upon this momentous era as a time when, beyond many, many individual contributions, two remarkable men shaped South Africa's destiny.

The first man is Nelson Mandela.

Literally millions of words have been written in praise of his vision, his strength, his unbending principles and his extraordinary spirit of reconciliation. Indeed, some of them have appeared earlier in these same pages.

I would simply add that, in my mind, one of Madiba's great qualities is his absolute selflessness. Throughout his life, in the fight against apartheid, in prison and then in power, he has suppressed his own needs beneath the needs of the nation. There are many thousands of examples, but perhaps the most recent was the manner in which, during April and May 2004, he defied his doctor's orders to play a decisive role in the closing days of the campaign to host the FIFA World Cup in 2010.

South African bid officials had identified the votes of the three FIFA Executive members in North America as pivotal and, in their final push for support, they asked Mandela to attend the CONCACAF Congress in Grenada. He agreed, boarded yet another plane and led the ultimately successful effort to win the votes.

Two weeks later, Mandela agreed to travel again, this time to Zurich where he introduced South Africa's final presentation to the FIFA Executive. It was highly appropriate that, the following day, he should be present when victory was announced.

In the past decade, I have been fortunate to work closely with Madiba on many issues, from the debate surrounding the Springbok emblem to various matters relating to the Olympics.

"Sam," he would say. "What do you think, Sam?"

Relentlessly cheerful, extraordinarily humane in his approach to every problem, genuine and beholden to nobody, he has become a worldwide icon for peace and freedom. As South Africans, we are all immensely privileged to call him our compatriot.

The second man is Thabo Mbeki. I first met our President in the early 1980s when, as the ANC's Press and Publicity officer in exile, he came to stay at Aziz Pahad's flat in north London. Many times, we sat long into the night and discussed the struggle and our campaign against apartheid sport.

In those times, he struck me as a highly intelligent man who was never closed to other opinions but who was remarkably skilful in persuading you to accept his point of view.

He would take time to explain the background to every issue and, through an entirely logical process, he would frame his view in such a way that it seemed clearly correct. He never told anyone to agree with him; he gently led them to that conclusion.

His exceptional ability to address issues and carry people with him in applying a solution took him to the top of the ANC and, when he took over the Foreign Affairs portfolio in the late 1980s, I worked very closely with him.

We became firm friends and, in many respects, I now regard him as my brother, as well as my President.

At stages, various observers have tried to compare him with Mandela, often expressing reservations about Mbeki.

There will never be another Mandela, not in a hundred years, not ever. He is a unique man who played a unique role, uniting the country. He set the bold agenda of reconciliation, and crystallised the dream and symbols of a new South Africa.

Mbeki's historic challenge is different; his task is to deliver change, to devise the mechanics and make it happen, to alleviate poverty, build houses, create jobs and stimulate growth.

As he makes progress, his philosophy is sometimes construed as being oblivious to whites. This is a gross misrepresentation. He has always been fully committed to inclusivity. I believe the day will come when historians reflect on his record of achievement, and the contemporary misgivings will have dissolved.

There is no rivalry between the two because they come from different generations. Govan Mbeki, the President's father, was a close friend and colleague of Mandela. So, when they appear in public together, there is no tension: Mbeki naturally defers to an elder and Mandela easily defers to 'our President'.

In many ways, their relationship echoes the alliance between Gandhi and Nehru in post-independence India.

Mandela, like Gandhi, has become the icon who conceives the dream; and Mbeki, like Nehru, has become the man who sets about the enormous task of putting the dream into action.

On June 12th, 2004, just six weeks before our team was due to leave for the Games in Athens, the Olympic flame arrived in South Africa from Cairo, Egypt, and was brandished for a day in Cape Town before continuing on its journey to Rio de Janeiro.

This flame represents the spirit of Olympism.

Several months before the opening of each Olympics, a flame is kindled in Olympia, the ancient home of the Games in Greece, by reflecting the natural rays of the sun from a mirror.

The flame is then carried to the host city without being extinguished, borne through country after country. It finally arrives at the stadium during the Opening Ceremony, where it burns brightly for the duration of the Games.

For the first time ever, in 2004, it was arranged that the flame would pass through all five continents en route to the Games.

Through an exciting and emotional day, the flame was carried in turn by a succession of eminent South Africans... Gert Potgieter, who competed at the 1956 Olympics in Melbourne, Francois Pienaar, captain of the World Champion rugby team in 1995, Penny Heyns, double gold medallist at Atlanta in 1996, George Bizos, South Africa's respected human rights lawyer, and others.

Most memorably, Nelson Mandela held the torch on Robben Island, where he had spent so long as a prisoner.

The South African leg of this global journey concluded when Lucas Radebe, the hugely popular footballer, carried the flame to light a furnace on Grand Parade, in Cape Town.

Finally, the flame was returned to the safekeeping of officials from the Athens 2004 Organising Committee and, at that moment, because no country is permitted to retain the flame, the furnace on the Grand Parade needed to be extinguished.

After a day filled with cheering and hullabaloo, the dying of the light suddenly, and quite unexpectedly, prompted a moment of complete silence and tangible sorrow.

I sensed people around me were moved. I was.

At that moment, something became clear to me.

If we are fortunate, a flame burns deep within each of us. It warms us with its heat, and it shows the way with its light; it moves us to strive for achievement and to persevere in adversity, to make sacrifices, to progress and do something worthwhile.

In my life, I have been doubly lucky.

A flame blazed within me when I went into exile and started to campaign against apartheid in sport, and a second flame has been burning within me for the past 14 years, when I have worked to implement equal opportunities in South African sport.

For this, I am grateful; and, as I watched the Olympic flame flicker, shrink and die that evening in Cape Town, I suddenly realised that, even now, after all the problems and solutions, after all the great days and bad days, after all the projects and campaigns, the flame still burns within me.

INDEX

167